# Don't Fix Me, Fix the Workplace

A Guide to Building Constructive
Working Relationships

PETER MILLS

GOKO
PUBLISHING

GOKO Management and Publishing
PO Box 7109
McMahons Point 2060
Sydney. Australia

First Edition

Library of Congress Cataloging-in-Publication Data
    Mills, Peter
    Don't Fix Me, Fix the Workplace

    p. cm.
    ISBN: 978-1-61339-888-3
    LCCN: 2016918407

# Acknowledgements

**I WISH TO** thank Barry and Sheila Deane, from PeopleFit Australasia, who developed the original Leadership Framework based on the work of Elliot Jaques and Lord Wilfred Brown. They have kindly given me full access to their substantial and excellent work, without which I could not have written this book.

I also wish to acknowledge Peter Dawe, a business studies teacher, and Therese Harris, a human resources manager, both of whom reviewed early drafts of the book and made valuable suggestions for improvement. Finally, I would like to thank my wife, Sue, who also reviewed the book and was a constant reference point, helping me to clarify my thoughts and ideas.

# Using This Book

**THIS BOOK PROVIDES** a holistic model for building constructive working relationships. It defines what organizations and managers must know and must do to create the working environment that enables the constructive working relationships that lead to productive work.

This book, like my previous book, *Leading People – The 10 Things Successful Managers Know and Do*, is based on The Leadership Framework, a holistic and integrated system of managerial leadership. The reason for using this management framework is that it considers the organization as a purpose-built structure, with systems of work and specifically designed working relationships that enable people to work towards a common business purpose. The Leadership Framework is specifically designed to enable productive work with constructive working relationships.

Being based on the same holistic framework, you will find there is some reiteration of concepts from the previous book, such as the expectations of all employees, the role of the manager, defining roles and building trust. In this book, however, this content is slanted towards building constructive working relationships. There is also substantial new material such as information on organizational structure, systems of work and the interpersonal skills and behaviors required of managers to build constructive working relationships.

*As all concepts are fully integrated, by the end of the book, the reader will have a strong understanding of the nature of people in a working environment and how to create a working environment that builds the trust required for constructive working relationships.*

At the end of each chapter, there are "Tips for Getting Started." These tips will help you on your journey to create a constructive working environment.

The companion website **www.theleadershipframework.com.au** offers additional free information and tools. You can also decide to join The Leadership Framework Network and gain access to all the information you need for a more comprehensive implementation.

# Contents

# Chapter 1

## The Need for a Different Approach

*Organizations with constructive working relationships are positive places to work. They have high-performance cultures with high levels of employee engagement.*

**CONSTRUCTIVE WORKING RELATIONSHIPS** are *where people work together in a positive manner, doing productive work to achieve organizational objectives.* Research continually shows that organizations with constructive working relationships are seen as great places to work. Such organizations are more likely to have high-performance cultures with high levels of employee engagement. They also:

- Attract and retain highly skilled staff.
- Have lower absenteeism.
- Have fewer cases of fraud.
- Have better safety practices with less bullying and harassment leading to reduced workers' compensation costs and insurance premiums.

People in these organizations are more likely to support organizational change and tend to be more innovative and creative, which gives such organizations a competitive edge.

For managers and their teams, having constructive working relationships provide additional benefits. Instead of spending time and energy overcoming problems associated with negative relationships, the focus is on achieving business goals. Day to day, work is more enjoyable, and the team is happier, more satisfied with their lives and feel healthier.

With constructive working relationships, managers get the best out of their team and out of others and achieve their outcomes, often with better results. They also assist others in the organization to do the same.

Having the whole organization working together, in a constructive manner, is good for individuals, customers, suppliers and key stakeholders. It is essential for business success.

So why don't all organizations have the constructive working relationships that enable productive work?

Having had significant experience in senior human resource roles, dealing with CEOs, managers, and individuals, I have seen and experienced first hand the way people work together and the way relationships can fall apart. Even with the best intentions and effort from all parties, working relationships can and do fail. This strains not only the people involved but also the working environment of their co-workers. I have seen whole divisions that, for the most part, refuse to work together, even at the senior level.

When trying to resolve these issues, organizations, CEOs, their top leadership teams and managers often talk about culture, so they target organizational values or behaviors. However, time and time again the focus moves to the individuals involved and not the working environment that created conflict in the first place.

Managers then try to "fix" people by giving them training on interpersonal skills. Sometimes this works, but more often than not it fails, as the working environment continues to be the source of frustration and irritation. Consequently, relationships never get back on track and continue to negatively impact productive work.

Part of the reason for this is that the current trend is to focus on the individual rather than fix the working environment that created the problem in the first place. If you search the internet using the phrase "building constructive working relationships," you will find a plethora of information about behaviors. This reflects the focus on interpersonal skills. There is very little information on the organizational requirements or managerial requirements to create a work environment that both enables and supports constructive work. This has resulted in an overemphasis on the symptoms without looking at the causes of work-related conflict.

Conflict at work often occurs when people are unable to perform their work or when expectations are not met. This then manifests itself in the use of poor behavior by one or both parties. The causes of failure are often due to things outside the control of the individual or groups concerned. These causes include unclear work boundaries, poor definition of work, ineffective systems of work, poor task assignment and differing expectations of outcomes or required service levels, all of which lead to a reduced ability to perform work effectively. In these circumstances, the focus of the individual often moves from what is best for the organization to behavior that says "I will do what is good for me and my mental state and my survival."

If the causal factors are not changed, the conflict will remain unresolved, may reoccur or the individual concerned will develop workarounds, often to the detriment of the organization. Furthermore, team members may inappropriately seek protection and support from others, thus creating third parties to the manager-employee relationship and increasing the conflict. Third parties in this context include other managers, human resources staff, and unions. Both outcomes hinder the development of positive working relationships and are unacceptable for a high performing business.

What is needed is an approach that considers the whole working environment, not an assumption that something is wrong with the individual, while leaving the causes of the poor behavior unattended. It requires a clear understanding of the working environment that shapes behavior. It needs a model for constructive working relationships based on specific understandings of people at work.

## Key Concepts

- Constructive working relationships are where people work together in a positive manner, doing productive work to achieve organizational objectives.
- Research continually shows that organizations with constructive working relationships are seen as great places to work. People in these organizations are more likely to support organizational change and tend to be more innovative and creative.
- People working in constructive working environments are happier, more satisfied with their lives and feel healthier.
- Having the whole organization working in a constructive manner is good for individuals, customers, suppliers and key stakeholders.
- Conflict at work often occurs when people are unable to perform their work or where expectations are not met. This manifests itself in the use of poor behavior by one or both parties.
- While the causes of failure are often due to things outside the control of the individuals or groups concerned, often the assumption is that something is wrong with the individual, leaving the causes of the poor behaviors unattended. If the causal factors are not changed, then conflict will remain unresolved, may reoccur or the individual concerned will develop workarounds, often to the detriment of the organization.
- What is needed is an approach that considers the whole working environment with specific understandings of people at work.

## Tips for Getting Started

1. Think about your working relationships. Are there areas where the relationship can be improved? What are the frustrations? What do you think are the causes? Write them down. After reading each chapter from chapter 4 to the summary, write down possible actions you can take to make the relationship more constructive.

2. Think about a member of your team who has a poor working relationship with you or with others. What do you think is driving their behaviors? What frustrates them and you? Write them down. After reading each chapter, from chapter 4 to chapter 10, write down possible actions you can take to make the relationship more constructive.

**An introduction to The Leadership Framework is available as a free download. Visit** www.theleadershipframework.com.au

# Chapter 2

## The Work Environment and People

*To build constructive working relationships requires an understanding of the nature of working organizations and people in the working environment.*

**TO BE ABLE** to build constructive working relationships, managers need to understand the working environment in which all employees find themselves. They need to understand "the working organization" that creates the working environment. In this way, they can focus on the cause and effect of people issues.

Managers also need to understand the nature of people in a working environment, how and why they react in the way they do. Only then can they take appropriate action to change the environment to enable the constructive working relationships that lead to productive work.

### What is a Working Organization?

Working organizations exist to coordinate the work of many people towards a common business purpose, that is, to produce the organization's products and service. Although working organizations have physical assets, they consist of people whose interaction is essential. The context of this interaction is defined by the organization's strategy and delivered through the organization's structure (functions, roles and role relationships) and its systems of work (policies, processes and information and communication technologies). These are in turn activated by the application of effective managerial leadership. Each component provides the context for people's work and creates the day to day working environment of all employees, including managers (see diagram below).

## The Working Organization

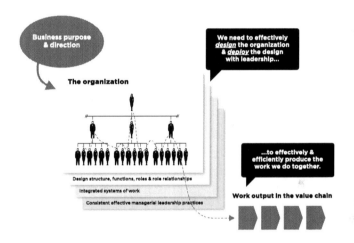

In defining the working organization, we can see that four interacting parts create its outputs:

i.   Purpose and Direction

The direction of a working organization, and therefore the context of the work for each person, is defined by the orga-nization's purpose and strategy. An organization's purpose and direction provide the focus and context for all work. The strategy specifies what the organization does and does not do. This results in initiatives designed to achieve defined organizational objectives that are what the organization is attempting to accomplish over a period of years, as represented by the organization's collective objectives.

Without this focus, the context of people's work will be confused, and unproductive work will occur. There will be a lack of prioritization of projects and a waste of time, effort, and resources. There will be confusion on what is important to the organization, and therefore people's day to day work. This resultant confusion will affect working relationships across the organization.

ii. Structure, Functions, Roles and Role Relationships

In order to deliver the organization's purpose and strategy, roles are created and organized into functions. This organizational structure provides the shared understanding of accountability and authority that exists between people whose work must be aligned and integrated with other roles to deliver the organization's products and services in line with the strategy. Each role has a specific purpose with specific accountabilities and authorities that enable people to work together effectively and collaboratively. These roles are commonly represented on paper as a two-dimensional organization chart.

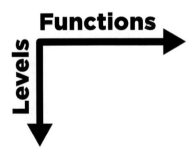

**Structure, levels of work, functions**

- The horizontal dimension defines how the work is organized into core functions such as sales, service and manufacturing and how it is supported by specialist functions such as finance and human resources.
- The vertical layers reflect levels of complexity of work and that work in organizations occurs over differing time periods, with each layer adding value in a different way.

If well designed the right work will be performed at the right level by the right roles and each role will have clear accountabilities with matching authority to complete their work. People will work in both a constructive and productive manner. If poorly designed there will be gaps or duplication of effort, there will be misaligned accountabilities and authorities for work. This has the potential to cause unnecessary conflict.

iii.  Systems of Work

Systems of work are the organization's policies, procedures, processes and information and communication technologies. They provide standardizing methods for work to be done to deliver the organization's products and services. They enable roles to work together, within teams, across teams and the organization. They enable roles (people) to work together to deliver the organization's purpose.

If well designed and aligned with requisite managerial leadership, systems of work help create the work environment that enables constructive working relationships and productive work. When poorly designed or poorly implemented, they will cause confusion and conflict.

iv.  Effective Managerial Leadership

Structure and systems of work are activated and deployed through effective leadership practices. Managers at every level are accountable to achieve the business goal set for them in line with the organization's strategy.

Managers:

- Set the purpose and direction for their team and enable team members to move together in that direction with competence, commitment, and enthusiasm.
- Build a team that is capable and committed to achieving business outcomes.
- Provide an environment that allows their team to be effective and satisfied in the work while developing their full potential.

Each part of the working organization must operate effectively to ensure the development and delivery of the constructive working relationships that lead to productive work. Without an effective structure, with appropriate functions, roles, and role relationships and without integrated systems of work, all activated by effective managerial leadership practices, the organization's strategy, and purpose may not be delivered, and the causes of failure will not be clear. Focus will be on individuals as the cause of failure and not the working environment created by the working organization.

## People in a Working Environment

As stated in the section "How to Use this Book," The Leadership Framework, a fully integrated set of principles and practices for managing people in a working environment, is the basis of this book's concepts. Importantly, the Leadership Framework contains specific beliefs about people in a working environment. These beliefs are that:

i. People are naturally motivated to work; they are not intrinsically lazy.
ii. People are social beings, and work is an environment where social interaction is required to achieve business outcomes.
iii. Organizations and their employees share a common goal in the need for productive work.

iv. The work environment critically influences an individual's ability to do their best work.
v. Productive work is enabled by systemic trust and fairness and is reduced by fear.
vi. People seek to work at a level in which they can use their capabilities to the fullest.
vii. People seek fair differential pay for that work.

Extrapolating these beliefs means:

- People come to work to do the best job they can, but their natural motivation to work and their performance effectiveness is affected by workplace conditions, that is, the working environment created by the working organization. If the conditions in the workplace are such that they induce confusion or fear, people cannot be expected to contribute fully.
- Work is a social environment where social interaction is required to achieve business outcomes. A clear understanding of the "social norms" and the "rules of engagement" are essential for people to work together effectively.
- Constructive working relationships cannot be built without trust. If the working environment does not create trust, then people will not work together constructively or work together effectively.
- Human beings are naturally social creatures — we need positive interactions. It makes sense that the better our relationships are at work, the happier and more productive we're going to be.
- People want to work at a level where they can use their capabilities to the fullest. If their role or tasks in a role do not match their individual capability, they will become frustrated or bored. This will have predictive consequences.
- Someone effectively contributing to their role expects fair payment for the work they do. People paid at equitable

levels feel satisfied, and pay tends not to be raised as a focusing issue in their workplace.

With an understanding of people at work and the working organization, managers can establish the workplace conditions that enable the constructive working relationships that lead to productive work.

## Key Concepts

- To be able to build constructive working relationships, managers need to understand the working environment in which all employees find themselves. They need to understand the working organization. They also need to understand the nature of people in a working environment.
- Working organizations exist to coordinate the work of many people towards a common business purpose, that is, to produce the organization's products and service.
- Although working organizations have physical assets, they consist of people whose interaction is required to deliver the organization's purpose. This interaction is defined by the organization's strategy and delivered by the organization's structure (functions, roles and role relationships) and its systems of work (policies, processes and information and communication technologies), all of which are activated by the application of effective managerial leadership.
- Strategy, structure, systems of work and managerial leadership provide the context for people's work and creates the day to day working environment of all employees.
- Without an effective structure, with appropriate functions, roles, and role relationships and without integrated systems of work, all activated by consistent and effective managerial leadership practices, the organization's strategy and purpose may not be delivered, and the causes of failure will not be clear.

- This book uses The Leadership Framework as the basis for the model for constructive working relationships. The Leadership Framework has seven assumptions about people and work. These are:
  o People are naturally motivated to work; they are not intrinsically lazy.
  o People are social beings, and work is an environment where social interaction is required to achieve business outcomes.
  o Organizations and their employees share a common goal in the need for productive work.
  o The work environment critically influences an individual's ability to do their best work.
  o Productive work is enabled by systemic trust and fairness and is reduced by fear.
  o People seek to work at a level in which they can use their capabilities to the fullest.
  o People seek fair differential pay for that work.
- With an understanding of people at work and the working organization, managers can set the workplace conditions that enable the constructive working relationships that lead to productive work.

## Tips for Getting Started

1. Consider the nature of working organizations. How does it relate to your organization or department? Think about how the working organization impacts your team.

2. One of The Leadership Framework's beliefs about people is, "The work environment critically influences an individual's ability to do their best work." Identify what aspects of the work environment critically impact your teams working relationships?

## Additional information available at
## www.theleadershipframework.com.au

1.  "Why Managers Fail" — available as a free download on The Leadership Framework website.
2.  Implement business strategy
3.  Design the organization
4.  Design and maintain productive systems of work
5.  Role of the manager
6.  Understand the role of others

# Chapter 3

## Setting Conditions for Constructive Working Relationships

*Building constructive working relationships
requires the creation of the right working
environment. This goes beyond the use of good
interpersonal skills.*

**ONE OF THE** Leadership Framework's beliefs about people at work is that "People are social beings and work is an environment where social interaction is required to achieve business outcomes." It makes sense therefore that the use of good interpersonal skills (by everybody) will assist in establishing more constructive behaviors and will provide some "social glue." However, interpersonal skills have limited value in a workplace and a working relationship which is otherwise flawed in its design or subject to ineffective leadership. To have constructive working relationships requires a working environment that both enables it and sustains it.

To build the constructive working relationships that lead to productive work, managers need to consider the whole working organization. They need a model that considers the interaction of people in a working environment, the environment that impacts every employee, every day.

## Model for Constructive Working Relationships

The model below incorporates all elements of the working organization, and The Leadership Framework's seven beliefs about people at work is embedded into each element (See Chapter 2: The Work Environment and People).

The basis for collaboration is built on the organization's structure, clearly defined roles and role relationships and the organization's systems of work, all of which is activated by effective managerial leadership, which includes the manager's day to day work.

### Model for Constructive Working Relationships

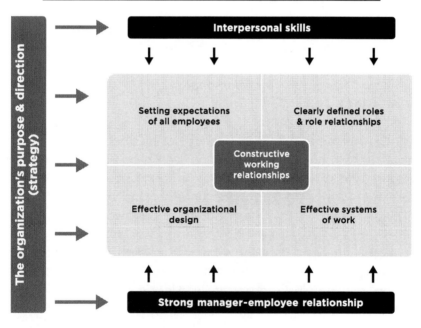

The model for constructive working relationships has six independent but interrelated parts. The context for each part of the model is defined by the organization's purpose and direction (strategy). These six parts are:

i.  Setting Expectations of All Employees

In organizations, all employees are expected to deliver the outputs required of their role and use the resources and processes specified by the organization. Expectations, however, go beyond this. As work is a social environment, where individuals are using their capability in a goal-directed manner, standards on *how* people are to work together is essential.

The requirements to enable constructive working relationships are defined in Chapter 4: Setting the Expectations for All Employees.

ii. Effective Organizational Design

An organization's design provides the shared understanding of accountability and authority that exists between people whose work is aligned and integrated to deliver the organization's purpose and direction. Effective design enables constructive working relationships while poor organizational design has the potential to create workplace conflict.

The requirements to enable constructive working relationships are defined in Chapter 5: Effective Organizational Design.

iii. Clearly Defined Roles and Role Relationships

In organizations, there are different types of roles. There are leadership roles, of which there are five types, specialist roles with six possible types of authority and team member roles. Well designed roles, with clear accountabilities and authorities, provide the rules for engagement and enables focused thinking about the work to be done. They enable people to work together both constructively and productively, towards business goals.

The requirements to enable constructive working relationships are defined in Chapter 6: Clearly Defining Roles and Role Relationships — Specialist Roles.

iv. Providing Effective Systems of Work

Systems of work, such as policies and processes enable people to work together. Systems of work create custom, practices, traditions, beliefs and assumptions, which in turn help create the organization's culture. Systems of work reinforce what is valued in the organization by the senior leadership team; therefore, their design is essential to enable constructive working relationships.

The requirements to enable constructive working relationships are defined in Chapter 7: Creating Effective Systems of Work.

v.  Strong Manager-Employee Relationships

The foundation of having constructive working relationships is the manager-employee relationship. A strong manager-employee relationship can only be achieved where managers have strong, personally earned authority gained through effective performance in their role. The focus of this relationship is on achieving business goals. It is based on care, dignity, respect and mutual trust between the manager and each team member and is critical to the success of both the manager and each team member.

The requirements to enable constructive working relationships are defined in Chapter 8: Building Strong Manager-Employee Relationships.

vi.  Interpersonal Skills

As people are social beings and work is an environment where social interaction is required to achieve business outcomes, managers need relationship management skills for dealing with people and managing issues. The development of these skills provides the "social glue" for the team to work together.

The requirements to enable constructive working relationships are defined in Chapter 9: Interpersonal skills.

A detailed explanation of each part of the model for constructive working relationships is in the following chapters.

## Key Concepts

- The work environment requires social interactions to achieve business outcomes. The use of good interpersonal skills (by everybody) will assist in establishing more constructive behaviors and provide some "social glue."
- Interpersonal skills have limited value in a workplace and a working relationship which is otherwise flawed in its design or subject to ineffective leadership.
- The context for each's person's work is defined by the organization's purpose and direction.
- To have constructive behavior requires an environment that both enables it and sustains it. This environment is created by:
  - Setting the expectations for how all employees should work together
  - Providing effective organizational design
  - Clearly defining roles and role relationships
  - Providing effective systems of work
  - Developing interpersonal skills
  - Building strong manager-employee relationships
- Embedded into the model for constructive working relationships are the Leadership Framework's seven beliefs about people in a working environment.

## Tips for Getting Started

1. Consider the working organization and discuss this model for building constructive working relationships with:
   a. Your manager and get feedback
   b. Your peer managers and get feedback
2. Consider how this model for constructive working relationships works for you and your team.

# Chapter 4

## Setting the Expectations for All Employees

*Work is an environment where social interaction
is required to achieve business outcomes. A clear
understanding of the social norms and the rules
of engagement are essential. Where the rules
for interaction are not clearly specified, they will
develop regardless.*

**THE FIRST STEP** in building constructive working relationships is to set expectations on how people are to work together. This includes ensuring behaviors such as honesty, integrity, respect for others, and collaboration are embedded in these expectations, so they become the social norms for the organization. If expectations are not set, then "the way we work around here" will still develop, as this is the nature of people in groups who have to interact.

In organizations, all employees are obliged to deliver the outputs required of their role and use the resources and process specified by the organization. Expectations, however, go beyond this. There are standards or expectations of behavior on how people are to interact to achieve business outcomes.

Although team members are not accountable for each other's work, all employees have an accountability to do their best and to work together to achieve outcomes. While many organizations have values, few clearly articulate how people are to work together. They may value teamwork or collaboration and use words such as, "We all have to work together," "We need to collaborate more effectively," or "We must have constructive behaviors," however, few organizations define what this looks like and even fewer hold their people to account for delivery.

So how can these constructive behaviors be defined in a meaningful way, in a way that all employees can understand?

To work together in a constructive manner requires all employees to:

- Fulfill commitments made
- Bring their full capability to work
- Continue to develop their performance effectiveness
- Provide their manager with feedback
- Work together productively.

These requirements are expanded in the table below.

## Expectations of All Employees

| Expectation | |
|---|---|
| Fulfill commitments made | • Deliver in-full on-time all their output commitments and expect the same of others. This includes commitments made across the organization to other individuals or departments<br>• Uphold the organization's values<br>• Under no circumstances should they "surprise" their manager on the delivery of output commitments. |

| | |
|---|---|
| Bring their full capability to work | • Apply their knowledge, skills and experience fully and effectively<br>• Exercise their discretion to deliver outcomes fully and appropriately<br>• Try different ways to achieve objectives even in difficult circumstances<br>• Work cooperatively with others to solve problems and share information within the context of the role<br>• Work within set policies, systems and procedures — refer to a higher level where appropriate<br>• Accept and adapt to change. |
| Continue to develop their performance effectiveness | • Work to improve their personal effectiveness in their role by actively participating in people management processes such as goal-setting and development. |
| Provide their manager with feedback | • Actively engage with their manager when tasks are assigned<br>• Look at ways to improve by providing feedback to their manager on tasks, systems and processes used<br>• Refer problems that cannot be resolved to their manager for assistance<br>• Immediately notify their manager if they are unable to achieve assigned task output (quantity, quality, time or cost). |

| Work together productively | • Work together to solve problems within the context set by their manager<br>• Persuade each other to act in a way that facilitates their work, to accommodate each other's needs as far as possible without changing or compromising their accountabilities or agreed/allocated objectives<br>• Do what is right for the function and the organization, even when this may cause a potential difficulty for their area<br>• If there is disagreement, they act as their manager would want them to, before escalating to their manager<br>• If agreement cannot be reached, they must escalate to their immediate manager who will either clarify the context and make a specific trade-off decision. |
| --- | --- |
| Limitations | • Should not tell each other what to do<br>• Should not stop each other from taking action<br>• Should not fight about who is right, but focus on the issue<br>• Should never speak negatively about their colleagues<br>• Team members are not accountable for each other's work and do not make judgments about each other's personal effectiveness. This is the role of the manager. |

Adapted from Elliott Jaques

The delivery of these expectations will reduce the causes of conflict and enable people to work together constructively. For these constructive behaviors to become habits requires constant communication of the requirements, with the manager holding each team member to account for their delivery. This communication can be done informally through feedback to team members or formally through the organization's performance management process and appraisal, reward, recognition and fair treatment systems of work.

To embed these *expectations of all employees* also requires the manager to role model the required behaviors in their day to day work. Failure to do so will mean that team members will believe that the expectations are optional, or the manager will lose respect — or both.

## Managers Working with their own Manager

Everyone is an employee of the organization and everyone has a manager. Managers do not lose their employee accountabilities when they move into a managerial role; they gain the additional accountabilities of a manager. Therefore, all managers have at least two sets of role accountabilities:

- One as the manager of their team, and
- Another as an individual employee reporting to their manager as outlined in the above *expectations for all employees*.

When working with your manager, you must continue to deliver *the expectations for all employees* to your manager. Therefore, for your manager, you must continue to:

- Fulfill commitments you make.
- Bring your full capability to work.
- Continue to develop your performance effectiveness.
- Provide your manager with feedback.
- Work together productively (with everyone).

In this way, a constructive working relationship will develop between you and your manager.

## Managers Working with Peers

When working with your peer managers, the expectations of all employees continue to apply, particularly the accountability to *work together productively*. That is to:

- Work together to solve problems within the context set by your manager.
- Persuade each other to act in a way that facilitates your work, to accommodate each other's needs as far as possible without changing or compromising your accountabilities or agreed/allocated objectives.
- Do what is right for the function and the organization, even when this may cause a potential difficulty for your area.
- If there is disagreement, act as your manager would want you to, before escalating to your manager.
- If agreement cannot be reached, escalate to your manager who will either clarify the context and make a specific trade-off decision.

In this way, the organization works together to achieve business outcomes, and constructive working relationships are maintained.

## Accountabilities for Setting Expectations

The CEO, with input from the senior leadership team, is accountable to decide the required *expectations of all employees* for the organization, as it is the CEO who decides the culture required for the organization to be successful.

Each and every manager is accountable to:

- Ensure team members understand these expectations
- Require their application on a day to day basis
- Hold team members to account for their delivery
- Role model the expectations

At the individual level, every person in the organization is expected to understand and fulfill the expectations.

## Now What?

While setting expectations on how people are to work constructively together is a good first step, it is only the beginning. The organization's senior leadership team and each and every manager must create the working environment that enables all employees to work together constructively and productively. This working environment is created through:

- Appropriate organizational design
- Clear roles and role relationships
- Productive systems of work
- Effective managerial leadership with a strong manager—employee working relationships using good interpersonal skills.

These requirements are covered in the following chapters.

## Key Concepts

- Although team members are not accountable for each other's work, all employees have an accountability to do their best and to work together to achieve business outcomes.
- The first step in building constructive working relationships is to set expectations on how people are to work together. If expectations are not set, then "the way we work around here" will still develop as this is the nature of people in groups who have to interact to achieve business outcomes.
- All employees must:
  o Fulfill commitments made
  o Bring their full capability to work
  o Continue to develop their performance effectiveness
  o Provide their manager with feedback

- o   Work together productively.
- For managers working with their manager, they must deliver the expectations of all employees to their manager.
- For managers working with peer managers, the expectations of all employees apply, particularly the accountability to *work together productively.*
- The accountability for deciding the required *expectations of all employees* for the organization is the CEO, with input from the senior leadership team. It is the CEO who decides the culture required to be successful.
- Each and every manager is accountable to:
  - o   Ensure team members understand how they are expected to work together
  - o   Require their application on a day to day basis
  - o   Hold team members to account for their delivery
  - o   Role model the expectations.

## Tips for Getting Started

1. Discuss your effectiveness in the delivery of the *expectations of all employees* with your manager.
2. Communicate the *expectations of all employees* to your team members and hold them to account for delivering them.

## Additional resources available at www.theleadershipframework.com.au

1. Manager role, accountabilities and authorities
2. Acting manager role, accountabilities and authorities
3. Supervisors/team leader's role, accountabilities and authorities
4. Team member role, accountabilities and authorities

# Chapter 5

## Effective Organizational Design

*The structure in which people
find themselves strongly influences their
behavior at work.*

**EFFECTIVE ORGANIZATIONAL DESIGN** is an essential ingredient to enable people to work together in a constructive and productive manner. Structure provides the shared understanding of the accountability and authority of how work is organized and delivered. Organizations, however, often get structure wrong, as they have no clear methodology for its development, try to follow other organization's structure, or go by trial and error. This often results in:

- Too many divisions
- Unclear accountabilities and authorities
- Duplication of effort
- Mixed functions
- Too many vertical levels of hierarchy
- Work being performed at the wrong level
- Employees having multiple managers, such as in matrix management systems
- Too many meetings with little outcome
- Lack of freedom to think
- The creation of low value or no value work

- Managers not adding value to the work of their direct reports
- Boring, unchallenging and unsatisfying roles
- Promotion to the next level is seen as a title change with no real meaning.

As structure is a driver of behavior, getting it wrong can create an environment that results in negative behaviors such as:

- Undermining
- Micro managing
- Workarounds
- Empire building
- Job protection.

Such behavior results in a loss of trust in the organization, a loss of confidence in the management system and frustration around the ability to get work done. It impacts the ability of people to work together and creates a working environment the encourages behaviors that hinder the constructive working relationships that enable productive work.

Two of The Leadership Framework's beliefs about people are that:

i. People are naturally motivated to work, and
ii. Organizations and their employees share a common goal in the need for productive work.

If the structure hinders their work, employees will get frustrated or work around it. This is not good for the organization or its systems of work. It is not good for working relationships.

## Issues in Organizational Design

Organizational design commences when the strategy to deliver the organization's purpose is clear. The first job of the CEO is to *organize* the work to be done. As shown in the following diagram, this involves grouping similar types of work together—the horizontal dimension and organizing work into different levels of complexity—the vertical dimension. The design of both the horizontal and vertical dimensions' impact working relationships.

## Dimensions of an Organization's Structure

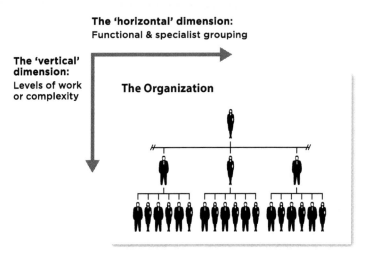

A 'map' of our working relationships...

## A. The Horizontal Dimension — Grouping, Separating, and Integrating Work

In designing the horizontal structure, the main issue is what work needs to be put together and what should be separated? There are three broad types of horizontal functions:

i.   Core operational functions such as production, sales, and service
ii.  Specialist support/service functions such as finance, human resources, and information technology
iii. Governance and control functions such as audit.

The grouping and separation of these types of functions will vary from organization to organization. A simple rule is that all work should remain embedded in the core functions and managers should retain control i.e. accountability and authority of all people, physical and financial resources to execute the core work in a continuous process flow unless:

- The complexity of the core work increases to require specialization
- Non-critical, enabling work, such as employee administration, can be cost effectively separated or sourced elsewhere
- The benefit of separating the work from the core function exceeds the extra effort of managing the added complexity of integrating the separate work. That is to say, only separate work from the core into support where the value created is greater than the effort of reintegrating the work
- The specialist work provides a competitive advantage or efficiency gain to the organization if separated from the core for a specific purpose.

Examples include:

- Creating a shared service function for non-core work such as administration work
- Creating an information technology function to enable cross-organizational integration
- Creating a research function due to the complexity of the work.

Each organization needs to make its decision based on its strategy, size, complexity and business requirements.

In the horizontal structure, conflict tends to be at the handoff points, where work crosses from one function to the next, for example, from marketing to sales.

Issues often relate to accountability and authority, resourcing and systems of work. Unless this work is properly aligned, silos will develop and workarounds will occur. Functions may start duplicating the work of other divisions to achieve outcomes. Alternatively, employees will try to resolve issues by developing personal relationships across functional boundaries. They will start swapping favors to get work done. New employees, who have not had time to establish long-term relationships, will get frustrated as they try to deliver their work. Clearly, this is not acceptable. It is the work of the CEO to integrate the work of the functions by clearly outlining the accountabilities and related authorities for the work.

While it is important to integrate the work for all divisions, a common issue for many organizations is the integration of the work of corporate specialist functions with that of core functions. Typical issues are:

- What is the role of the specialist function?
- What are the specialist function's accountabilities and authorities?
- How do they integrate with manager accountabilities and authorities?

For example, in people management issues, what is the role of the human resources function and what is the role of the manager?

- If there is a people management issue, who is accountable to fix it?
- If there is corporate training on bullying and harassment, as a manager, do I have to send my team members, because I don't think it is an issue in my department?
- A manager wants to give a certain pay increase, but HR says no.

These are common questions in organizations and often create conflict, not just between the corporate function and the manager but also between managers and their team members.

To enable constructive working relationships, the accountabilities and authorities of core and corporate specialist function must be clear. The functions must be designed to align with their counterpart roles using appropriate accountabilities and authorities. As previously stated, it is the role of the CEO to set each functions accountabilities and authorities.

So what are appropriate accountabilities for corporate specialist functions?

To be effective, the relationship between corporate specialist functions, line managers, and their teams must be linked to the nature of the work. Corporate specialist functions exist due to an organizational need for specialist knowledge, skills, and experience. Therefore, corporate specialist functions must be accountable to *develop* the organizational strategy for their specialist function. The corporate specialist function creates and then *recommends* this strategy to the CEO and leadership team. The *"decide authority"* is performed by the CEO with *input* and *feedback* by the leadership team.

Corporate specialist functions must also be accountable to *design* the systems of work to support the approved strategy for the specialist area.

When implementing accountabilities for any function, it is important to remember the role of the manager. The role of the manager is to *achieve the business goals set for them and at the same time, provide an environment that allows their staff to be effective and satisfied with their work while developing their full potential.* For this reason, *implementation* is led by each manager for his/her team, in line with corporate requirements. The role of the corporate specialist function is to provide *advice* and *support* to the line manager.

Typical accountabilities and authorities for specialist corporate functions are defined in the table below.

## Comparisons of Accountabilities of Corporate Specialist Functions and Line Roles

| Typical Accountabilities and Authorities for Corporate Specialist Functions | | |
|---|---|---|
| Element | Corporate Specialist Functions (e.g., safety, HR, finance, IT) | Line Manager Roles CEO, executive team, managers |
| Strategy | • Develop and recommend the (specialist) strategy, e.g., IT strategy, finance strategy, HR strategy, safety strategy, communications strategy, marketing strategy *Typically uses advisory and coordinating authorities* | • Decide organizations strategy<br>• Input to discipline strategy, e.g., IT, finance, HR, safety<br>• Decide cross-functional strategies, e.g., IT, finance, HR, safety, communications, marketing |
| System of Work Design | • Design and recommend the (specialist) system or process aligned with business strategy *Typically uses coordinating authorities* | • Input to the design<br>• Decide the system |

| System of Work Use | Deliver service to enable managers to use the system in their areas, e.g.:<br>• Provide specialist services, e.g., recruitment, procurement<br>• Provide training services<br>• Provide advice on the use of the system<br>• Coordinate activities to enable systems use<br>*Typically uses advisory, coordinating, and monitoring authorities* | • Lead the implementation, using the system as authorized<br>• Initiate services within the agreed context of the function or system<br>• Review and assure performance to system (by own team)<br>• Decide trade-offs within systems limits<br><br>*Typically uses service getting authorities* |
|---|---|---|
| Governance: Control, Monitor, Audit | • Collate and analyze data on compliance and quality<br>• Recommend improvements<br>• Recommend corrective action<br>• Report against measures<br>• Action authorized system changes<br>*Typically uses monitoring and audit authorities* | • Provide data for reporting<br>• Provide feedback on system effectiveness<br>• Decide corrective action<br>• Implement corrective action in own teams<br>• Decide system changes |

*These "authorities" are defined in Chapter 6: Clearly Define Roles and Role Relationships — Specialist Roles*

As can be seen from the table, line manager roles and corporate specialist roles are complementary. They should not be in conflict. What is required is a clear understanding of the accountabilities and authorities of these complementary relationships. Essential to this process is to embed the accountabilities and authorities for strategy development and approval, of ownership of systems of work and governance and control requirements, in the organization's systems of work (see Chapter 7: Effective Systems of Work).

With a clear definition and understanding of the work and each functions accountabilities and authorities, organizations can design roles, role relationships, and systems of work that support the constructive working relationships that enable productive work, not create inbuilt conflict caused by poor organizational design and alignment.

Understanding, engaging with and respecting the role of others, with their legitimate accountabilities and authorities, allows managers to work effectively in the organization and enables the development of constructive working relationships within their team, across other teams and the organization.

## B. The Vertical Dimension — Creating Levels of Work

Before looking at the vertical structure, it is important to understand the nature of work in organizations. According to Dr. Elliott Jaques, work is a mental process. It might be associated with physical things, such as, fabricating, repairs or digging a hole, but it is the internal mental process that people use quite naturally to figure out the problems in a task and to solve them. The work that a person does is about making decisions and acting on them. It is an *exercise of judgment,* and in doing this, people apply their intellect, their knowledge, skills, and experience to the problem.

According to Jaques, the vertical structure of an organization is a series of levels where the complexity of work or the *exercising of judgment in making decisions and acting on them,* occurs at different levels over distinctly different time frames. Each level adds value in a different way. Jaques called these levels "stratum."

Organizations will vary in the number of levels or stratum required due to their size, their nature and, the complexity of their business. However, the type of work at each level is the same.

The first three levels in an organization, called stratum I, II and III, are concerned with *doing* work. This work may consist of buying, selling, providing services or products. This is where most of the organization operates — planning the work, implementing the work and executing the work.

The next two levels, stratum IV, and V, move away from concrete activities to those which are more complex, often abstract, and represent progress by degrees over longer periods of time. These levels are the executive levels of the organization. It is where continuity of operations is maintained while the organization follows its strategic intent to a desired future. The time from concept to completion is longer. For example, for the CEO of a Stratum V level organization, the time from developing a strategy to being able to assess the success of the strategy is five to ten years. The strategy may include developing new products or technologies or finding and developing new markets, including mergers and acquisitions.

The next two levels (Stratum VI and VII) are that of multinational or international corporations and international bureaucracy. Here decisions are made on multinational and global issues of resource allocation, integrated profit and loss statements and decisions where and in what to invest or divest and when and why. They are concerned with integrated thinking across diverse fields.

The table below shows the levels of work in a typical five-level organization, with each level adding value in a unique way.

## Examples of Levels of Work

| Stratum level | Time Span | Type of Work | Typical Roles |
|---|---|---|---|
| V | 5 to10 years<br><br>Immediate results are not available to verify results. The more complex decisions create a point of no return. Choices made can result in loss of value to shareholders. | **Develops strategy**<br><br>Business direction and deliver the organization's purpose: *Ensures that an overall strategy is continually developed and refined to maximize the value that the organization delivers to stakeholders.* | • Managing director<br>• CEO<br>• Division of a multinational organization |
| IV | 2 to 5 years<br><br>Up to 5 years before the outcome of tasks can be assessed and before the benefits or otherwise are realized. | **Integrates the work**<br><br>Executing strategy and systems improvement: *Designing system improvements to optimize long-term outcomes to maximize stakeholder value.* | • General managers<br>• Vice presidents |
| III | 1 year to 2 years<br><br>Up to 2 years before the most complex task can be completed and the fruits of the decision can be seen and judgment confirmed. | **Plans the work**<br><br>Sustaining operational delivery of function: *Ensuring that the key processes are under control to sustain delivery of outputs which contribute to the achievement of outcomes over time.* | • Managers of managers |

| | | | |
|---|---|---|---|
| **II** | 3 months to 1 year<br><br>Impacts of decisions can take up to 12 months to become apparent. | **Implements the work**<br><br>Team leadership and process performance:<br>*Manages trends and input consumption and control processes to achieve those outputs consistently.* | • Frontline Manager<br>• Lawyers<br>• Accountants<br>• HR professionals<br>• Tax specialists |
| **I** | 1 day to 3 months<br><br>Failures in judgment become apparent quickly. The outcome of actions can be more or less predicted with accuracy. | **Executes the work**<br><br>Skilled production and output:<br>*Completes tasks assigned, adhere to defined procedures. Monitors processes and report on anomalies.* | • Operator level<br>• Electrician<br>• Manual laborer<br>• Call center staff<br>• Sales Representative<br>• Barista<br>• Personal assistant |

Another way of looking at levels of work is shown in the diagram below. The diagram highlights the different types of thinking, at different levels of complexity, over different periods of time in a five-level organization.

## Complexity, Time Span & Organizational Work

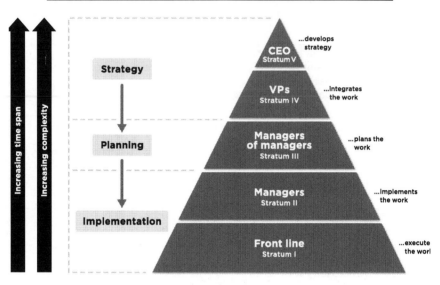

In this example, the five levels of work are organized into three broad categories:

i. Strategy development: those who develop the strategy and integrate the work to deliver it — Stratum levels IV and V

ii. Planning the work: those who plan the work — Stratum level III

iii. Implementing or doing the work: those who implement the work and execute it —Stratum levels I and II.

So how can the vertical levels of work affect working relationships?

A key principle of organizational design is a vertical level of management must only be created where the work is more complex than the work of the role below. This not only ensures that the right work is performed at the right level by the right people, but it also ensures that each level of management can add value to the roles immediately below. The reality is that organizations cannot function effectively if a level is missing, partially present or overlaps with other levels. If any of this occurs there are predictable consequences:

- If there are too many levels, work will become too confined with not enough room for decision making.
  - o Managers will have a lack of freedom to think, with too many people checking and cross checking work. It encourages micromanagement.
  - o Managers will build more and processes and policies to control what is irrelevant.
  - o Organizational strategy will be lost, and communication across the organization will become difficult. To overcome this, organizations often create or enhance communications departments to do what should be managerial work.
  - o Managers will not add value to the work of their team as they will be operating at a similar level.
  - o The unique value add of roles will be unclear with overlap and duplication.
  - o Accountabilities and authorities will likely be blurred and fuzzy, yet everyone is busy.
  - o Work will not be challenging or satisfying.
  - o More and more meetings will occur, and it will not be clear who is accountable for the outcomes as authority is not clear.
  - o Direct reports may skip a level in order to have issues resolved.
  - o Internal politics will be intense and who is accountable for what will be an issue.
- If a work level is missing, that is, where manager positions operate at more than one stratum level higher than their direct reports, there will be a lack of traction in getting action on strategies or plans.
  - o Managers may not articulate concepts, strategy, goals and tasks at a level of detail that their direct reports can action. Objectives may be unclear as there is no context and little prioritization.

- o The managerial leader will often have to dip down to fill the missing work level, and this is unsatisfactory for all parties.
- If a role is stretched across multiple work levels its unique value add will be confused or unclear. It is likely the role authority will not match its accountabilities, and it will be trying to deliver too much to too many. This will disempower direct reports, and this will, in turn, disempower the work levels below. It may result in bottlenecks, hasty or inappropriate decisions and changing priorities.

Whether the organization has too many levels or roles are compressed or work levels are missing or stretched across multiple levels of work, the outcome is the same. It creates an environment where conflict can occur. This is not the fault of the people involved. It is a predictable outcome of an environment in which people are trying to do their best but are unable to do so.

Ensuring vertical levels align with the different levels of complexity of work not only ensures work is performed in a constructive manner it, enables productive work.

## Accountabilities for Organizational Design

The board of directors or the owner of the business:
- Defines the purpose of the business, so that value is delivered to customers and stakeholders.
- Approves the strategy and then delegates the accountability (with appropriate authority) to the CEO to take the organization in the direction set to deliver the strategic objectives and to establish the conditions necessary to ensure the effective delivery of value.

The CEO authorizes:

- The principles and guidelines to create the organization structure, including accountabilities and authorities for design and deployment.
- The functions the organization needs, i.e., divisions.
- The roles that directly report to those functions, i.e., direct reporting roles to the VP/general manager roles.
- The total number of levels in each division.
- The total number of roles (positions) in each division.

The CEO, with the executive team, aligns the work between each function and ensures that:

- A set of organizational design principles and guidelines is established to inform the design and deployment of structure in the organization.
- All managers at all levels have a working understanding of the principles and guidelines for organizational design.
- All managers understand their particular accountabilities and authorities in relation to design and deployment of structure.
- The whole organization and each of its parts have minimum-but-sufficient levels of management.
- A consistent approach is taken to design divisions, departments and front-line output teams across the organization.

To support the above, the head of human resources, as the custodian of the organizational design system, provides advice, monitors, and reports on all organizational and role design issues.

Managers of managers:

- Integrate the work of their team of teams and ensure collaboration across their part of the organization.
- Apply managerial leadership to align departments, ensuring effective systems of work and assuring the planned work is delivered effectively.

- Decide on how many subordinate roles their managers will have and at what level these roles are positioned.
- Design roles — agree on the structure of the team below and ensure roles are appropriately placed for the complexity of work required.
- Monitor cross-organizational collaboration between their part of the organization and other parts and works with their peers and their immediate managers to ensure that cross-organizational work flows smoothly.

Managers — every manager at every level must:
- Build and lead an effective team so that each member is fully committed to and capable of moving in the direction set. When the direction or a system of work changes, they are accountable to lead change in their team. This includes change to the organization structure.
- Ensure every role adds value to the business and has a documented and authorized purpose, accountabilities, authorities, and identified key role relationships.
- Ensure every employee is appointed to a role where their capability is assessed as a good fit for the role.
- Recommend and implement approved structural changes.
- Decide what tasks they assign to their team members.

## Key Concepts

- Effective organizational design is an essential ingredient to enable people to work together in a constructive and productive manner. Structure provides the shared understanding of the accountability and authority of how work is organized and delivered.
- In the horizontal structure, the area of conflict tends to be the handoff points, where work is transferred from one function to the next. Issues often relate to accountability and authority,

resourcing and systems of work. It is the work of the CEO to integrate the work of functions, clearly outlining the accountabilities and related authorities for the work.

- Line manager roles and corporate specialist roles are complementary; they are not meant to be a source of conflict. What is required is a clear understanding of the accountabilities and authorities of their complementary relationships.

- For corporate specialist functions, it is essential to ensure the accountabilities for strategy development, ownership and use of systems of work, and governance and control are clearly specified and embedded in the organization's systems of work.

- An organization's vertical structure is a series of levels, with different types of work being performed in each level and with each level adding value in a different way. A vertical level of management must only be created where the level of work is more complex than the work of the role below.

- Unless work levels are structured to reflect the level of complexity, the required outcomes will not be achieved, and working relationships will break down.

- Organizations cannot function effectively where a level is missing, partially present or overlaps with other levels. If this occurs, there are predictable consequences:
  o If there are too many levels, work will become too confined with not enough room for decision making. The role will be compressed, so the unique value add of the role will be unclear with overlap and duplication. Authority and accountabilities will likely be blurred and fuzzy, yet everyone is busy.
  o If a work level is missing, there will be a lack of traction in getting action on strategies or plans. The managerial leader will often have to dip down to fill the missing work level

o   If a role is stretched across multiple work levels, its unique value add will be confused or unclear.

## Tips for Getting Started

1.  Select a corporate specialist function such as human resource or finance in your organization. Using the table Comparisons of Accountabilities of Corporate Specialist Functions and Line Roles in this chapter, assess if the accountabilities for strategy development, systems of work and governance are clear. Using this information assess if the work of core functions and specialist functions have been aligned and integrated. Discuss your findings with the relevant corporate function.

2.  Using the table Examples of Levels of Work assess if the type of work in your role is one level of complexity above your direct reporting roles? How do you know this?

## Additional information available at www.theleadershipframework.com.au

1.  The organizational design sequence
2.  Principles for organizational design
3.  Accountabilities and authorities for organizational design
4.  What is work?
5.  Description of levels of work
6.  What is individual capability
7.  Matching accountability with authority
8.  Designing effective roles
9.  Selecting the right person for a role

# Chapter 6

## Clearly Define Roles and Role Relationships – Specialist Roles

*Organizations have extensive networks of people
working together, and unless there is a clear
understanding of the legitimate nature of these
working relationships,
work will be inefficient, and conflict can occur.*

**WHILE ALIGNING EACH** function in an organization is essential to enable constructive working relationships, so too is the alignment of roles. This is especially important for specialist roles.

Line manager roles and specialist roles are different. A line manager is accountable for the output and behavior of their team and, as such, has the authority to assign tasks directly to team members. Manager roles are the only roles that can assign tasks to their team members, and a manager is the only person who can hold their team members to account for their individual performance effectiveness.

Specialist roles, such as technical specialists and planners, exist to support managerial work. They are critical to the effectiveness of the working organization. These roles support the line by providing expertise or specialist services. Specialist roles cannot assign tasks to a manager or the manager's team members, but they are authorized to do specific work. Specialist roles have authorities to initiate tasks or provide services on request, but cannot directly assign work to others through a direct reporting relationship. Specialist roles can be thought of as *horizontal* working relationships.

Issues often arise when team members do not have a clear understanding of the nature of a specialist's separate, but complementary work. To avoid conflict, it is essential that specialist roles are effectively designed and that their role relationships, i.e., the role's accountabilities and authorities, are authorized and clear. These relationships must also be embedded into the organization's systems of work and communicated to the people whose roles are required to work together.

## Defining Specialist Working Relationships

A manager's role has three types of work:
- Technical work, such as delivering the core components of the role, completing the assigned tasks as part of the business plan and developing new methods.
- Programming work, such as planning and scheduling work, preparing budgets, monitoring progress and reporting.
- People work, which includes building productive working relationships, managing performance and integrating the work of their team.

Specialist roles are established to assist managers with elements of their technical or programming work; however, the manager always retains the accountability for work output.

Managers must never delegate their people management accountabilities to specialists, as the manager is the person who needs to maintain a strong manager — employee working relationship with each team member.

An example of a typical department with two specialists reporting to a manager is shown in the diagram below.

## Types of Work in the Role

### A manager's work has three dimensions:
- **People**
- **Technical**
- **Pr**ogramming

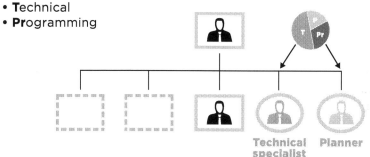

Technical specialist    Planner

A manager may delegate their Pr and T work - but must not delegate the leadership (such as, relationship and integration) component of the P work

Typical issues for employees working with specialists are:
- What is the role of the specialist?
- What are the specialist's accountabilities and authorities?
- How do they integrate with manager accountabilities and authorities?
- How do they impact with my accountabilities and authorities?
- How do they work with other team members?

These issues must be resolved in the role design process and not left for individuals to sort out for themselves. When managers create specialist roles, they must be designed for a specific business purpose with clear accountabilities and authorities for the specialist's work. These accountabilities and authorities must be within the manager's accountabilities and authorities. Importantly, the meaning of the authorities must be understood by all parties. For example, if a planner has the authority to *monitor* work it must be clear what monitor means. If a technical specialist provides *advice*, it must be clear what advice means. In the following diagram, a planner has authority to *monitor*, and the meaning of monitor is specified.

## Define Working Relationships

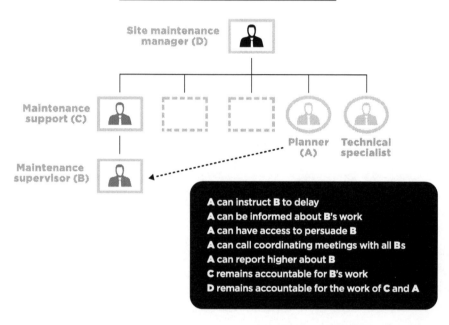

It is, therefore, essential that organizations define the types of authority that can be used and what each authority means. Assuming that within the *expectations of all employees* the requirement to collaborate is defined, there are six additional types of specialist role authorities. These are authorities to:

- o Advise
- o Get/Give service
- o Monitor
- o Coordinate

o  Audit
o  Prescribe

The six types of authorities for specialist working relationships are expanded in the table below.

## The Six Types of Specialist Role Relationships
### Advisory Authority

- Held accountable, by their manager, to provide unsolicited expert advice to identified roles to ensure that best practice is understood and considered for use. The Advisor is accountable for the quality of the advice.
- The recipient is accountable to consider the advice given. The recipient remains fully accountable for the decisions on what to do with the advice and for the work outputs to which the advice relates.

Example: a person who provides quality advice to a person they believe should be kept up to date, e.g., human resources officer.

### Service Getting/Giving Authority

There are two parts to this relationship, the service getter, and the service receiver. A person can ask another to provide services as authorized by their manager and within the scope of the role of the service giver.

- Service **getters** must have clearly specified what services they are authorized to get and from whom
- Service **givers** need to know what services they must provide and to whom.

If the service giver cannot provide the needed service for whatever reason, the service getter must take the matter higher to his or her manager.

Example: a person who, on request, provides authorized services within the agreed quality, quantity, time and resources e.g. a human resources officer.

## Monitoring Authority

A person monitors to ensure compliance with policies, systems, and standards relating to their area of expertise.
- The monitor has the accountability and authority to be kept informed of the relevant activities of the role being monitored.
- If the monitor judges that work outcomes are or could be non-compliant, monitors can instruct responders to delay to allow escalation to the responder's immediate manager/s.

Example: a person who needs to ensure that employees who do not report to them are adhering to policies and are sustaining adequate standards such as quality, e.g., quality assurance officer.

## Coordinating Authority

Assists a line manager with programming work, by gathering and analyzing group/team resources, e.g., technical, and people and financial, developing group plans or budgets to assist the optimal use of resources.
- Provides and explains plans and other tools to enable a group or team to work together effectively in a joint undertaking
- Keeps group informed of progress in carrying out the tasks
- Helps overcome setbacks

The group members' manager assigns the planned activities and re-directions.

Example: a person who gets a number of colleagues to agree on joint action or the synchronizing of work, e.g., product development coordinator.

## Audit Authority

This authority is used to keep the quality of processes within control limits by giving the auditor authority to stop a person from doing something, e.g., working outside quality specifications.

- Can inspect the work in accordance with corporate procedures
- Responders must stop, and can escalate later

Example: a person who instructs someone to stop doing something and they must stop doing it. Only used in safety or risk critical circumstances. Unlike prescribing, they do not have the authority to instruct another to do some other type of work, e.g., internal auditor.

## Prescribe Authority

This authority is used only in circumstances of extreme risk to the business, e.g., critical and high-risk safety situations.

- This requires a person to do something and that person must do or stop doing something as specified by the prescriber.
- The person being asked to take action can escalate the issue later.

Example: a person who can instruct another person to perform tasks. Only applies to safety or risk critical circumstances, e.g., safety officer.

These authorities are summarized and compared in the table below where A is the initiator and B is the responder

## Summary of Specialist's Role Relationships

| Role Components / Accountabilities & Authorities | Advisory | Service Getting/ Giving | Monitor | Coordinate | Audit | Prescribe |
|---|---|---|---|---|---|---|
| A can instruct B to do something | - | ✓ | - | - | - | ✓ |
| A can instruct B to stop & B stops | - | - | - | - | ✓ | ✓ |
| A can instruct B to delay & B delays | - | ✓ | ✓ | ✓ | ✓ | ✓ |
| A and B disagree. A decides | - | - | - | - | ✓ | ✓ |
| A can be informed about B's work | - | - | ✓ | ✓ | ✓ | ✓ |
| A can have access to persuade B | - | - | ✓ | ✓ | ✓ | ✓ |
| A can have access to explain to B | ✓ | - | ✓ | ✓ | ✓ | ✓ |
| A can call coordinative meeting with Bs | - | - | - | ✓ | - | - |
| A can report higher about B | - | ✓ | ✓ | ✓ | ✓ | ✓ |
| If A and B disagree, the do what their immediate manager would want | - | ✓ | - | ✓ | - | - |

Note that a specialist's authorities should be set at the minimum level required to perform the tasks in the role. Furthermore, some roles will combine a number of these authorities into one role for different types of work.

Failure to specify the accountabilities and authorities for specialist roles creates the working environment for conflict and will have predictable consequences:

- Politics, with the related poor behaviors, may emerge, undermining the organization's effectiveness or corrupting its values.
- Employees will need to rely on the goodwill of their peers to get work done.
- Time and resources will be wasted in "sorting out" the work.
- Workarounds and unauthorized systems of work will be developed as people will still want to achieve their objectives outside the authorized system of work.
- The specialist manager will not be able to hold the specialist to account for their personal effectiveness because the specialist is likely to be trying to deal with ineffective working relationships and may not to have clear authority to act.

## Accountabilities

To enable constructive working relationships, line managers who have specialist roles reporting to them must integrate those roles with other roles. It is not up to individuals to "work out" or to "discover how" they are to work together to achieve business outcomes. This is a clear accountability of the manager.

Managers with specialist direct reports must:
- Ensure the specialist's role accountabilities and authorities are clear and that they are understood by their counterparts in the organization, including the requirement to collaborate and how to proceed in the event of a disagreement.
- Ensure work processes are documented, communicated to and understood by all who work in the process.
- Monitor the specialist's work, the quality of his/her collaboration with counterparts, provide meaningful feedback and coach for improved effectiveness.
- Identify early signs of conflict and act to resolve it productively.
- Collaborate with counterpart managers to resolve issues that cannot be resolved by the direct report.

- Escalate problems that cannot be resolved to the next level manager, e.g., the crossover manager.
- Ensure that their direct reports performance on collaboration and conflict resolution is reviewed as part of his/her performance review.

Line managers working with specialist roles must be clear on the specialist's accountabilities and authorities of those roles and respect them. If the accountabilities or authorities are not clear, then they must discuss this with the specialist's manager.

Understanding, engaging with and respecting the role of specialists, with their legitimate accountabilities and authorities, allows roles (people) to work together effectively and enables the development of constructive working relationships within the team, across other teams and the organization.

## Key Concepts

- One of the biggest relationship issues managers have in an organization is working with specialists such as technical specialists and planners. This usually occurs when the parties do not have a clear understanding of the nature of their separate but complementary roles, accountabilities, and authorities.
- Line manager roles and specialist roles are different. A line manager has the authority to assign tasks directly to their team members. Specialist roles are roles that support the line by providing expertise or specialist services.
- Specialist roles cannot assign tasks to a manager or the manager's team members, but they are authorized to do specific work.
- Specialist roles may be established to assist managers with elements of their technical or programming work, not their people work.

- The relationship between specialist roles, line managers, and their teams is specific and linked to the nature of their work or function. There are six different types of specialist authorities some of which may be combined into one role. These are:
  o Advisory Authority
  o Service Getting/Giving Authority
  o Monitoring Authority
  o Coordinating Authority
  o Audit Authority
  o Prescribe Authority
- Line managers who have specialist roles reporting to them must integrate those roles with other roles and ensure the specialist accountabilities and authorities are not only set but also communicated and understood by all relevant parties.
- Line managers working with specialist roles must be clear on the accountabilities and authorities of those roles and respect them.

## Tips for Getting Started

1. If you are a line manager with a specialist role reporting to you, using the table, "The Six Types of Specialist Role Relationships" in this chapter, define the authorities of each specialist role. If they are not clear, discuss this with your manager and communicate how accountabilities and authorities of each relationship are to work with you and your team in the future.

2. If you work with specialists within your broader team, do you understand their authorities? If not, then clarify the authorities with your manager or the specialist or their manager.

# Additional information available at www.theleadershipframework.com.au

1. Matching accountability with authority
2. Designing effective roles
3. Detailed guide to authorities of specialist functions
4. Project manager role, accountabilities, and authorities
5. Committee role, accountabilities, and authorities.

# Chapter 7

## Effective Systems of Work

*Roles (people) require effective systems of work —*
*policies, procedures,*
*forms and information and communication*
*technologies —*
*to enable them to work together in a constructive*
*and productive manner.*

**SYSTEMS OF WORK** exist to coordinate and direct the work of many people to deliver the organization's products and services. Systems of work bind work together and were well designed and aligned with requisite managerial leadership; their influence is highly positive. They help build trust in the organization, support constructive working relationships and enable productive work. If a system of work is poorly designed, it may not be used or be misused, and its influence will be counterproductive. This not only impacts work outputs, but it also creates unnecessary work conflict and reduces organizational trust.

Systems of work:
- Provide the *standardizing* methods and boundaries for work to be done.
- Facilitate work across functions, across teams and within teams.

- Align people and work with legislation, social norms, and the organization's values.
- Allow the executive team to monitor and verify that the organization's purpose is being achieved in accordance with the cultural, ethical and moral standards set by the organization.

Systems of work have four main components — inputs, a process, outputs and feedback mechanisms. These components are shown in the following diagram.

## Components of a System

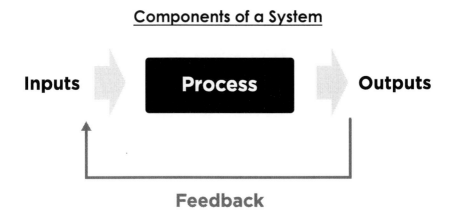

Inputs → **Process** → Outputs

### Feedback

Each component contains a set of interrelated and interacting elements such as policies, procedures, forms, information and communication technologies. Examples of systems of work and their associated subsystems include:

- The People Management System. This system allows for the effective management of people and includes processes to develop the organizational structure, create roles, select and induct new employees, assign and assess work, reward and develop people and provide fair treatment.
- The Procurement Management System. This system ensures effective procurement of goods and services. It includes processes to research procurement options, develop a

procurement strategy, develop procurement documents, invite responses, evaluate responses, form a contract and manage delivery.

To support the development of constructive working relationships managers must have a clear understanding of the nature of systems of work and their impact on people, work, and organizational culture. Managers must also understand the key principles for designing and reviewing systems of work so they can create a work environment that builds systemic trust, enables constructive working relationships and productive work.

## Systems and Day to Day Work

Two of The Leadership Framework's beliefs about people and work are:
  i.   The work environment critically influences an individual's ability to do their best work.
  ii.  Productive work is enabled by systemic trust and fairness and is reduced by fear.

Systems of work are a key component of the day to day working environment for most employees. People not only work in the system, but they also interact with it, and it interacts with them. Therefore, systems of work critically influence the ability of people to do their best work. It is difficult for a manager to counter the impact of bad systems.

Common conflict points for systems of work are where:
  • Handover points are not clear.
  • Incorrect or incomplete inputs are received from others that delay or impair work.
  • The system does not do what it is supposed to do.
  • The system is adjusted with little or no consideration for those who work in the system or those who rely on the system's outcomes.

- Accountabilities and authorities for the system or within the system are unclear.
- The work outputs are not used or not trusted.

All these issues impact the day to day work of employees. All these issues have the potential to cause frustration, friction, and conflict. Therefore, the design and deployment of systems of work are critical for organizational trust and constructive working relationships.

## Systems and Culture

Culture is the shared assumptions and beliefs a group of people has about certain behaviors based on what that group values or does not value. The more beliefs people share, the stronger the culture. Culture gives people a framework within which they can begin to organize their world and their behavior. Put simply; culture is the accepted standards of behavior, "the way things are done around here."

When people join an organization, they usually have worked in other organizations that may have had different standards and different expectations of their employees. These new employees bring their backgrounds, with a complete set of values, preferences, and inhibitors (VPIs), an innate level of work ability (LoWA) and their knowledge, skills, and experience (KSE) to their new organization. This occurs even if they come directly from school or university.

Employee behavior is impacted by:
- Managerial leadership practices/behavior
- The organization's systems of work
- The symbols created in relation to the above, such as recognition, uniforms, car parks and rewards

The following diagrams outline these impacts on employee behavior.

# Impacts on Employee Behavior

Note: In the above diagram organizational design
is part of "Systems."

An organization's leadership team defines and sustains its culture through what it values and embeds through the design and deployment of its rules, regulations, policies, procedures, and symbols. These are the things that create custom, practices, traditions, beliefs and assumptions and are a significant influence on how people experience work. They create standards and expectations on how work is done. The importance of systems of work in creating culture should not be underestimated. Leadership dependent on role modeling alone will not last as behavior will revert unless it is reinforced by a system of work.

This is because systems of work:
- Operate all the time, all day, every day. Unlike the manager, they are ever present.
- Reinforce what is valued in the organization.
- Are a major part of the work environment. They embed required behavior in processes and, as processes are repeated like habits, eventually, employees get used to them and act according to their requirements — "It's the way we do things around here."

When well designed, systems of work are a key contributor to shaping constructive working relationships.

## Principles for Design of a System of Work

To help people work constructively, efficiently, consistently and within required limits, all systems of work must be:
- Easy to use in relation to the output they deliver
- Integrated and aligned with other related systems and processes (systems of work)
- Induce feelings of mutual trust and fairness — based on clear and fair principles and rules
- Produce predictable outcomes and reliable results each time they are used.

When designed this way they will be used consistently by the managers and all other relevant employees.

To achieve this outcome, as a minimum, systems of work must include the following design principles:

### a) All systems of work must have a designated system owner

Every system of work must have a designated owner of the system (the *systems owner*). For any system of work, this is the crossover manager for all users of the system. This is because the crossover manager is the only role that:

- Can work across all related processes within the system, with the authority and experience to identify and implement necessary changes
- Has the authority to engage the whole team to understand and agree on the principles of the system, to assure it is fit for use and then to hold them accountable for input, implementation, and review
- Can understand and integrate all of the feedback loops and time delayed effects with the system
- Can ensure the system of work is used effectively across the whole area to which it applies.

Having the crossover manager as the systems owner ensures the whole system is considered when it is designed, or changes are made. In this way, decisions can be made on what is best for the total system of work, not just to satisfy a person or department.

For cross-organization systems, the crossover manager is the CEO.

To assist in fulfilling his/her, accountabilities systems owners may designate a systems custodian who will hold accountability for carrying out the work and who ensures appropriate engagement of users in the design and use of the systems. For example, the VP of Finance is often the custodian of the financial management system while the CEO remains the system owner.

**b) All systems of work must be designed to meet the needs of the customer/end user/beneficiary of the system**

As systems exist to deliver specified outputs for customers/end users/beneficiaries of the system work, these people/roles must be identified and their needs understood and specified.

This is important so that:

- The quality, quantity, and timeliness of system outputs can be determined
- Stakeholders can be advised or consulted when the system is altered or is to cease operation.

**c) All systems of work must be consistent with legislation, regulation and other corporate policies and standards**

All systems must be consistent with legislation, regulation, and the other corporate policies that reflect the organization's standards and values. For example, the development of a sales or production system must be consistent with other relevant organizational systems such as the People Management System, Safety Management System, Environmental and Quality Management Systems. Failure to do so would not only put the organization at risk and be inconsistent with organizational requirements; it would inevitably lead to conflict with those who work in other systems of work.

**d) The design of all systems of work must include the specification of working relationships**

Working relationships must be established between roles, not people (see Chapter 6: Clearly Define Roles and Role Relationships — Specialist Roles). Establishing clear role relationships enables work to be done and disagreements to be resolved. In establishing working relationships, the systems designer must specify the accountabilities and authorities for each role using the system of work. This will ensure clarity on issues around the systems inputs, processes, outputs and feedback mechanisms. This will reduce conflict.

**e) All stakeholders must be engaged in the development and use of the system**

All systems stakeholders must be consulted on its development and use. Where required, a user reference group can be created to provide input. This will not only ensure appropriate input and an appropriate level of consultation in the systems design; it will build trust and reduce the potential for conflict in the future. The systems designer and systems owner must consider all inputs, but the systems owner makes the final decision.

### f) All systems of work must equalize treatment of employees unless there is a business reason not to equalize

When looking at different systems of work, it is important to understand their intent. Is the intent to differentiate or to equalize? Systems of equalization treat people the same way. They do not differentiate between an operator, manager or the CEO. An example of this is a safety system. Irrespective of your position, title or rank, if you enter certain work sites, you must wear a hard hat and other required personal protective equipment. Systems that equalize promote organizational trust and fairness.

Systems of differentiation treat people differently. They distinguish between roles. For example, some roles may be paid based on commissions or bonuses while others are not.

All systems of work should equalize unless there is a clear work-related or business-related reason not to. If there is no such reason for a system which differentiates, that system and the managerial work associated, is likely to be seen by employees to be unfair and can be expected to diminish mutual trust in the organization. Unfair systems drive non-compliance and dysfunctional behavior.

### g) All systems of work must have evaluation and control built into the system design

Systems can only be maintained as authorized and productive systems if control and audit work is effectively established. Controls assure the correct use of the system.

Where possible, measures must also be established. These measures must be directly related to the purpose and outcomes of the system. They need to consider all aspects of the output — quality, quantity, cost, and timeliness.

For example, a recruitment system may have measures about its effectiveness, as in the example below.

## Example of Controls

| Control | Measure | Period |
|---|---|---|
| Example 1:<br>Recruitment<br>Quarterly<br>dashboard<br>(internal) | • Cost per hire<br>*(cost)*<br>• Time to fill<br>*(timeliness)* | Post recruitment<br>review<br>Quarterly report |
| Example 2:<br>Recruitment<br>End of probation<br>questionnaire<br>manager (internal) | • Quality of hire<br>against position<br>description and<br>key values/<br>behaviors<br>*(quality)* | 3 months after hire<br>(end of probation) |

### h) All systems of work must have a continuous improvement process build into the system design

All systems of work must be designed with feedback mechanisms. The systems owner/custodian is accountable to ensure suggestions are considered and changes authorized and communicated.

Using these eight basic design principles will not only improve productivity, but it will also improve organizational trust, the quality of the working environment and reduce unnecessary conflict.

## People Management Systems and Trust

While trust and fairness must be built into all systems of work, it is essential for people management systems. This is achieved by integrating the role of the manager-once-removed (MoR) as the basis for building trust in the system of management.

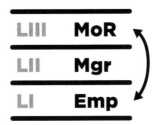

**The manager-once-removed
relationship**

In the People Management System, the role of the manager once removed is to:

i.  Ensure consistency and quality of leadership for their employee-once-removed (Emp). They do this by:

   o  Linking vertical and horizontal role relationships to ensure collaboration and alignment

   o  Coaching their direct report managers on their leadership effectiveness

   o  Shaping the workplace culture and setting expectations of behavior for all managers in the business unit

   o  Reviewing managerial decisions of their direct reports as part of performance assessment.

ii. Ensure fair treatment. They do this by:

- o Providing objectivity for decisions affecting their manager's team
- o Ensuring consistent application of policies across the business unit
- o Deciding appeal outcomes.

iii. Build capability. They do this by:
- o Bringing a wider perspective of the organization to identify future opportunities and role requirements
- o Designing structure for the employee-once-removed
- o Assessing the potential of the employee-once-removed for current and future roles
- o Deciding on promotion/demotion/dismissal of the employee-once-removed.

iv. Integrate the work of their team of teams. They do this by:
- o Setting the context for work of the business unit
- o Establishing systems of work that integrate the end-to-end processes of the business unit
- o Ensuring their managers collaborate constructively to achieve the overall plan of the business unit.

Integrating the MoR into people management systems brings a wider perspective to the people management issues of the organizations and creates systemic trust. Two of The Leadership Framework's beliefs about people are "The work environment critically influences an individual's ability to do their best work" and "Productive work is enabled by systemic trust and fairness and is reduced by fear." Building these accountabilities, with the appropriate authorities, into the organization's systems of work will increase organizational trust and fairness. For example, building the requirement for the MoR to review a direct manager's assessment of their team member's performance effectiveness or remuneration review improves the fairness of the system. This, in turn, improves trust in the organization and reduces the potential for conflict.

## Accountabilities for Systems of Work

Designing effective systems is complex work. It requires an understanding of the organization's purpose and objectives and the external and internal impacts on the business. It also requires the ability to ensure all systems of work produce the required outcomes and the integration of the organization's values. This is high-level work, therefore the accountability for the development of systems of work belongs to the CEO and the senior leadership team. Part of this accountability is to ensure that all systems of work conform to defined essential design principles.

The CEO is also the "owner" of all cross-organizational systems of work, and as such, may delegate specific accountabilities and authorities to selected general managers/vice presidents to assist with the essential work of initiating, analyzing, designing, implementing and reviewing systems of work. In performing this delegated work, the selected general managers are the "custodians" of the systems of work allocated to them. Generally, the system custodian will gather input for the purpose of formulating a recommendation to the system owner.

All managers are accountable to:

- Implement authorized systems of work in their area
- Discuss with their team on how to specifically apply the system in a work area
- Ensure the appropriate use of systems of work in their area
- Provide feedback to the system owner/custodian on the effectiveness of the system of work (using the systems feedback mechanisms)
- Monitor to ensure the system of work is used as intended in their area

Managers are not authorized to change a system of work without approval from the system owner/custodian.

All employees are accountable to:

- Work within set systems of work and refer issues to a higher level where appropriate
- Look at ways to improve by providing feedback to their manager on the systems of work used. Note that employees are not authorized to change a system of work without the approval of their manager, who requires the approval of the system owner.

(See Chapter 4: Setting Expectations of All Employees)

## Key Concepts

- A system of work is a framework that ensures a replicable set of activities to achieve a specific business purpose in line with the organization's values. They include a set of interacting and interrelated elements such as policies, procedures, forms, information and communication technologies.
- Systems of work:
  - o Coordinate and direct the work of many people towards a common purpose
  - o Provide the standardizing methods and boundaries for work to be done
  - o Facilitate work across functions, across teams and within teams
  - o Align people and work with legislation, social norms and the organization's values
  - o Allow the executive team to monitor and verify that the organization's purpose is being achieved in accordance with the cultural, ethical and moral standards set by the organization.

- Systems of work create the day to day working environment for most employees.
- Where systems of work are well designed and aligned with requisite managerial leadership, their influence will be highly productive. If poorly designed, not used or misused, their influence will be counter-productive and can cause conflict.
- While trust and fairness must be built into all systems of work, it is essential for people management systems. This is achieved by using the manager-once-removed as the basis for building trust in the system of management.
- To ensure all systems of work produce the required outcomes, they must conform to defined essential design principles. As a minimum all systems of work must:
  o Have a designated system owner
  o Be designed to meet the needs of the customer/end user/beneficiary of the system
  o Be consistent with legislation, regulation and other corporate policies and standards
  o Specify working relationships in the system of work
  o Engage all stakeholders in the development and use of the system
  o Equalize the treatment of employees unless there is a business reason not to equalize
  o Have a continuous improvement process build into the system design
- Designing effective systems is complex work. It requires an understanding of the organization's purpose and objectives and the external and internal impacts on the business. It also requires the ability to integrate what the organization values.
- Providing effective systems of work is a key accountability of the CEO and the Executive team.
- All managers are accountable to:
  o Implement authorized systems of work in their area

o Discuss with their team the application of each system in their work area
o Ensure the appropriate use of systems of work in their area
o Provide feedback to the system owner/custodian on the effectiveness of the system of work (using the systems feedback mechanisms)
o Monitor to ensure the system of work is used as intended
• All employees are accountable to:
o Work within set systems of work and refer issues to a higher level where appropriate
o Look at ways to improve systems of work by providing feedback to their manager

## Tips for Getting Started

1. Pick a system of work in your area. How do you know the process is operating effectively — what are the measures? What are the feedback mechanisms for the system of work?
2. Pick a system of work in your area and complete a systems scan. Identify areas for improvement. Note: a system of work Effectiveness Scan is available as a free download on The Leadership Framework website.

## Additional information available at www.theleadershipframework.com.au

1. Systems of work and culture
2. Trust and fairness — the role of the manager-once-removed
3. Ensuring the consistency and quality of leadership
4. Ensuring fair treatment and justice
5. Systems of work — roles, accountabilities, and authorities
6. Principles for design of a system of work
7. Process for designing or reviewing a system of work
8. Systems of work control document — template

9.  Example: System of work control document — people management system
10. Systems of work Effectiveness Scan

# Chapter 8

## Building Trust and Strong
## Manager-Employee Working Relationships

*To have constructive working relationships,
managers must build a strong, two-way,
trusting, working relationship with each team
member. The focus of this relationship
is on achieving business goals, with team
members working to their full potential.
This relationship is a working relationship, not a
social one.*

**CRITICAL TO THE** success of any manager is their working relationship with their team members. Managers must be able to trust team members, and each team member must be able to trust their manager.

Two of The Leadership Framework's beliefs about people and work are that:

1. The work environment critically influences an individual's ability to do their best work, and
2. Productive work is enabled by systemic trust and fairness and is reduced by fear.

If there is no trust and workplace conditions are such that they induce fear, people cannot be expected to do their best.

Trust, for this purpose, is defined as *the ability to rely on others to be truthful, to do as they say and to follow established rules, procedures and custom and practice.* It is a simple but clear definition that applies specifically to the workplace.

In delivering their role, all manager actions are viewed by their team members through the lens of trust and fairness — "Can I trust you? Can I trust that I will be safe in this workplace?"

Even the treatment of others is part of perceived trust. "Are people in this workplace treated fairly?"

The answers to these questions are key to the extent to which employees can commit both emotionally and rationally, in other words, heart and mind.

## Do I Trust You?

The importance of building trust for a strong manager-employee relationship should not be underestimated. Failure to do so may result in employees inappropriately seeking protection from others, thus creating third parties to the manager-employee relationship. Third parties in this context include other managers, human resources staff, and unions.

## Triangle of Relationships

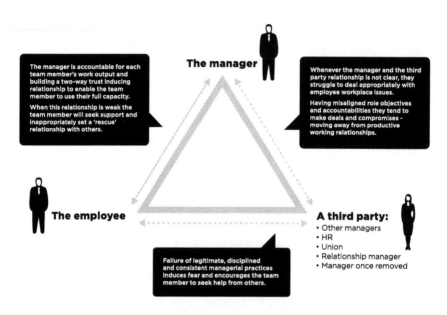

**The manager**

The manager is accountable for each team member's work output and building a two-way trust inducing relationship to enable the team member to use their full capacity.

When this relationship is weak the team member will seek support and inappropriately set a 'rescue' relationship with others.

Whenever the manager and the third party relationship is not clear, they struggle to deal appropriately with employee workplace issues.

Having misaligned role objectives and accountabilities they tend to make deals and compromises - moving away from productive working relationships.

**The employee**

**A third party:**
• Other managers
• HR
• Union
• Relationship manager
• Manager once removed

Failure of legitimate, disciplined and consistent managerial practices induces fear and encourages the team member to seek help from others.

This is not to say that employees do not have legitimate working relationships with other roles, both internal and external to the organization, they do. All of these working relationships, however, must be clear as to their purpose, objectives, and processes used. They must be aligned to ensure productive outcomes for the organization, manager and the individual employee. Doing so enables each party to properly and legitimately do their work to support the employee in a way that is appropriate and authorized.

Where there is an absence of effective managerial leadership and effective supporting systems of work, the possible good work of third parties will be limited. Their attempts to provide protection to the team member may further compromise working relationships, undermine mutual trust and reduce employee engagement as a third party is not accountable for the person's performance effectiveness, output or development in the role. Nor do third parties have authority to do the work to "put things right," to appoint to a role, assign work, review the individual's work or recognize good work and reward effort.

It is the manager's working relationship with each team member, based on trust; that will ensure success and build constructive working relationships.

So how do managers build the trust required to facilitate strong, two-way, working relationships with each team member?

Managers build trust through the effective delivery of their role. This means

- Demonstrating capability in their role
- Providing a safe place to work
- Consistently and fairly applying the organization's systems of work
- Continually engaging their team through communication of what is required for the business and why.

It is only when all four aspects are effectively delivered that the trust required for a strong manager-employee working relationship can develop.

## Demonstrating Capability in Their Role

To demonstrate capability in their role, managers need:

- Specific knowledge, skills, and experience. This goes beyond the technical and programming aspects of the manager's role. It includes the people management skills.
- To value their work and demonstrate trust-inducing behaviors
- A level of workability to add value to the work of their team

It is the unique combination of all of these factors that provide managers with the level of individual capability required to build strong manager-employee relationships.

i.    Knowledge, skills, and experience (KSE)

The role of the manager is to achieve the business goals set for them (by their manager). As managers achieve these goals through their team, managers must be able to:

*Build and lead an effective team, so that each member is fully committed to, and capable of, moving in the direction set.*

This is achieved through a manager's effective delivery of the performance management sequence of work. This sequence starts with effective role design, followed by selection for the role, then induction of the individual into the role and continues while the individual is working in the role. Each part of the sequence has a different emphasis with the same goal, i.e., having *fully-loaded* roles filled with people capable of doing their work. This sequence is shown in the diagram below.

**The performance
management sequence**

In this sequence:

**a) Role design** establishes the role, i.e., the role's purpose and objectives, its accountabilities and authorities and its working relationships with other roles. Effectively designed roles enable people to work together with freedom as they are clear about the work they have to do. They know the intended outputs and the boundaries in which to accomplish them. They know who has what accountability and who holds what authority.

b) **Selection** is to identify and appoint individuals whose capability is judged to best suit the capability requirements of the role. Using a transparent process establishes fairness and enables team members to feel confident in the decision. The selection process is also an opportunity to commence building a constructive working relationship with possible new team members.

c) **Induction** is to familiarize those selected about the work required for the role, its relationships with other roles and the incumbents in those roles. Also, they need to be familiarized with the systems of work which include the policies and work processes relating to the role, an overview of the typical tasks, the current priority tasks of the role and the performance requirements of the role. It is the first opportunity for the manager and new team member to start working together and to create a constructive working relationship. It also shows the new team member that the manager wants them to be successful.

d) **Assigning** and **assessing** work is a foundation condition for individual performance effectiveness. The manager monitors the individual as he or she progresses in work, providing feedback about the progress and how effectively the individual is working. This shows that the work the team member does is important and that the manager takes accountability for the output of the team.

e) **Development** in the role involves creating opportunities to coach the individual on how to be more effective, thus demonstrating that he/she is aware of the team members work and wants to support them to succeed.

**f)** **Reward** and recognize and as appropriate. The intent is to create conditions where all employees are in a position to see that the organization is a meritocracy — a place where people are paid fairly based on their performance effectiveness.

Each part of the *performance management sequence* is an opportunity to apply leadership and build trust — trust in the organization's system of work and trust in the manager.

To effectively lead their team managers, also requires specific interpersonal skills. These skills enable managers to handle their day to day issues, such as skills for addressing unacceptable performance or handling an employee complaint, in a trust-inducing manner. These skills are outlined in Chapter 9: Interpersonal Skills for Managers.

ii.   Values, preferences, and inhibitors

Values and preferences determine the types of work that individuals can do well, that is, what they are intrinsically motivated to do. To do their job well, managers need to value the work of a manager. Where an individual does not find value or enjoyment in a particular kind of work, they are unlikely to be able to sustain effort over time to excel in their role. If managers do not enjoy managing people, they will be unable to sustain the effort to build trust.

To lead in a trust-inducing manner, managers also need to demonstrate certain behaviors. A lot of research has occurred over the years to determine the behaviors required for leaders. In examining this issue through the lens of the Leadership Framework (see Appendix 1), we find there are four behavioral requirements for managers. These are:
- Honesty
- Integrity
- Respect for others
- Collaboration

There are specific reasons for this list, and they are based on The Leadership Framework's beliefs about people and the model for constructive working relationships. The behaviors of **honesty, integrity** and **respect** are the essential requirements to build trust. This trust is the basis for the strong manager-employee relationships that enable the constructive working relationships. Without these behaviors there can be no trust; without trust, a strong manager-employee working relationship cannot develop.

In relation to collaboration, managers do not work alone. They work in the context of a working organization. They have working relationships with their direct team and their manager. They also work across teams, with other managers and with people in specialist roles. To be effective, managers must work **collaboratively** with these roles to achieve the organization's goals. The basis for collaboration is built into the organization's structure (see Chapter 5: Effective Organizational Design), on role design with clear definition of role accountabilities and authorities (see Chapter 6: Clearly Define Roles and Role Relationships — Specialist Roles) and the organization's systems of work (see Chapter 7: Effective Systems of Work).

In delivering these behaviors, it is important that managers use their personal style. Often organizations seek to change the personality of managers. When this occurs, it usually fails as people are not able to maintain these changes over long periods of time. Alternatively, they seem fake to their team. Everyone is an individual and people need to work together within boundaries and guidelines, but they do not have to be the same. They do, however, have continually to demonstrate the behaviors of honesty, integrity, respect, and collaboration.

It should be noted that the behaviors of **honesty, integrity, respect** for others and **collaboration** are embedded in the expectations of all employees (see Chapter 4: Setting the Expectations of All Employees). For example, collaboration is embedded in the requirement to work productively together. Therefore, all employees, not only managers, are expected to demonstrate these behaviors.

Creating trust also requires an absence of negative behaviors. If a manager demonstrates extremes of behavior, such as aggression, bullying, harassment, drug and alcohol dependency, these behaviors will overshadow the good work a manager does and will reduce their effectiveness in the role. Trust will be diminished, and working relationships negatively impacted.

iii.  Level of workability (LoWA)

Level of workability is an individual's cognitive ability to assimilate data and information and to exercise sound judgment in the face of ambiguity and uncertainty. Matching an individual's level of mental processing ability with the complexity of tasks in a role is a minimum requirement to work effectively in a role. Therefore, manager roles must not only be designed at one level of work above the role of their direct reports (see Chapter 5: Effective Organizational Structure), the manager must have a LoWA matched to the tasks in the role. Otherwise, they will not be able to solve the problems of the role and may not even understand that there is a problem.

One of The Leadership Framework's beliefs about people is:

*People seek to work at a level in which they can use their capabilities to the full.*

When a person's individual capability matches the role requirements, the person feels satisfaction in being able to do their role well. They will be in flow — see diagram below.

## Matching a Person to a Role

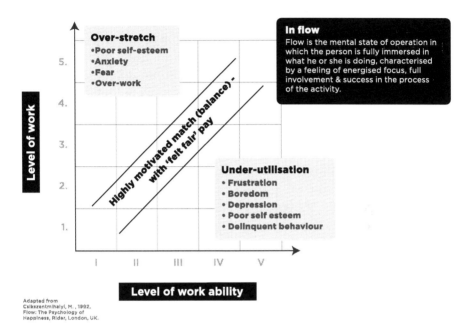

Adapted from
Csikszentmihalyi, M., 1992,
Flow: The Psychology of
Happiness, Rider, London, UK.

If a person is not in flow, there will be predictable consequences.

- If a person's LoWA is higher than the role, they will feel underutilized, or get distracted by trying to find work at a higher level to satisfy them.
- If a person's LoWA is lower than that required for the role, they will not be able to solve the problems necessary for the role and cannot, therefore, meet the role requirements. They will feel overworked and anxious. They will develop poor self-esteem.

A general principle is that people will grow or shrink their role and tasks to the level of work in which they are most comfortable to operate and in which they feel in flow. This applies to all roles at all work levels.

The more complex the role, e.g., CEO or VP/general manager, the greater the risk to the delivery of organizational outcomes.

When there is a mismatch between an individual capability profile and role requirements, it is detrimental to both the organization and the individual. It means that the work required in the role is most likely not being done effectively and that the person in the role feels either underutilized or overly stretched and may have poor self-esteem as a result. This will impact the working dynamics of the team and therefore impact working relationships.

In summary, where managers do not have the individual capability to do their role other behaviors develop. These unwanted behaviors will develop in the manager, in the manager's team members and even in others. The manager may unconsciously give away their leadership to others in their team who then become the de facto leaders. In some cases, team members or other managers steal the manager's leadership. Team members start questioning who the leader is and who is making the decisions. This is not good for the manager or team members. Team members need to respect the decisions managers make. If they cannot trust the decisions, they lose trust, and inappropriate behaviors develop. This isn't the fault of the individual. It is a natural reaction to the environment where people want to do good work but are not able to. It is up to the manager's manager to take corrective action and reset the working environment.

## Providing a Safe Place to Work

Managers must provide a safe working environment for their team. Besides any moral or legal obligation to do so, managers cannot build the trust required for strong manager-employee working relationships or expect productive work in an unsafe work environment. This not only includes providing a safe physical environment but also an environment free from bullying and harassment.

## Consistently and Fairly Apply Systems of Work

Managers must consistently and fairly apply the organization's systems of work. Consistent application of good managerial practices and systems of work builds trust. Every time a manager fails to apply a consequence for breaches of a system of work, the manager automatically creates new wider boundaries for their team members work performance. If the manager applies consequences to some team members and not for others, questions of favoritism or victimization will arise. This undermines trust.

Furthermore, if a manager personally fails to demonstrate the use of a system, this action is in effect "approving" non-compliance for team members as they continually evaluate the manager's behavior in all interactions. For example, if a policy prohibits team members from sharing passwords that access computer applications, but then the manager shares his/her password when information is required, this undermines both the system and the manager. It reduces trust.

## Continually Engaging Their Team

All employees want to be part of an organization's success, however, to do so they must personally be engaged in the organization. Engaging the team builds trust. As per The Leadership Framework's beliefs about people:

- Organizations and their employees share a common goal in the need for productive work.
- People seek to work at a level in which they can use their capabilities to the full.

To engage the team a manager must:

i.   Continually address the work interests of all employees

Managers must continually address the *four key questions* that all employees can be expected to have. These are:

1. Where are we going?
   (What is our direction? What are our priorities? What do we need to do to be successful?)
2. What's my role?
   (What is my part in this?)
3. How will my performance be judged?
   (How am I measured?)
4. Where am I going?
   (What is my future in the company? This last question is answered by the team member's manager-once-removed).

These questions are often answered through the organization's systems of work, for example, "What is my role?" is contained in position descriptions. "How will my performance be judged?" is in the performance appraisal system. However, managers must continually set the context for team members through both formal and informal processes on a day to day basis. Keeping the focus on the *4 Questions* engages each team member in their work and builds trust.

ii.  Create an inclusive culture

An inclusive culture can only happen when team members are kept informed by their manager on what is happening in the business unit and are provided with opportunities to be involved in the decision-making process. This is a genuine two-way process that does not merely take into account the input of team members but deliberately involves and engages them as a means to build trust, motivation and to ensure an optimum outcome.

This does not mean that it is a democracy where decisions are reached by a consensus or vote. It means that team members are encouraged to have an input and are heard. The manager, however, as he/she is accountable for the output of the team, makes the final decision.

iii.   Provide role clarity

Role clarity, with clear accountability and authority, builds individual confidence and esteem. It generates trust in the system of work.

Managers must ensure team members understand their role requirements, including the role's boundaries. This allows people to apply their knowledge, skills, and experience to achieve outcomes.

Role clarity extends beyond the tasks in the position description. It includes the broader accountabilities of all employees on how they are expected to work with their manager, their team and others in the organization. These expectations are to:
- Fulfill commitments made
- Bring their full capability to work
- Continue to develop their performance effectiveness
- Provide their manager with feedback
- To work together productively

The role of the manager is to ensure team members understand these expectations, require their application on a day to day basis and to hold each team member to account for their delivery in full.

Role clarity enables people to exercise judgment in making decisions. It enables them to use their capability. Role clarity enables empowerment.

## Accountability

The role of the manager is *to achieve the business goals set for them while providing an environment that allows their team to be effective and satisfied with their work while developing their full potential. To do this, managers must build and lead an effective team, so that each member is fully committed to, and capable of, moving in the established direction.* This outcome can only be achieved with strong, two-way, trusting, working relationships. Therefore it is the manager who is accountable to build these working relationships.

## Key Concepts

- Managers must build a strong, two-way, trusting, working relationship with each team member. The focus of this relationship is on achieving business goals with team members working to their full potential. Failure to build trust may result in employees inappropriately seeking protection from others thus creating third parties to the manager-employee relationship.
- Constructive working relationships can only occur in an environment of trust. If the conditions in the workplace are such that they induce fear, people cannot be expected to do their best.
- Trust in the workplace is defined as "the ability to rely on others to be truthful, to do as they say and to follow established rules, procedures and custom and practice."
- Managers build trust through:
  o Demonstrating capability in their role
  o Providing a safe place to work
  o Consistently and fairly applying the organization's systems of work
  o Continually engaging their team through communication of what is required for the business and why

## Tips for Getting Started

1. Hold a one-on-one meeting with each of your team members. In relation to their role, answer the first three of the four questions all employees have.
   a) Where are we heading (as a division or organization)?
   b) What is my role?
   c) How is my performance measured?
2. Improve your delivery of the performance management sequence of work. Read the book *Leading People — The 10 Things Successful Managers Know and Do* by Peter Mills.

## Additional information available at www.theleadershipframework.com.au

1. Trust, fairness and systems of work
2. Trust and fairness — the role of the manager-once-removed
3. Ensuring the consistency and quality of leadership
4. Ensuring fair treatment and justice
5. Creating effective roles and put good people in them
6. Assigning and assessing work
7. Building great teamwork
8. Improving team capability
9. Rewarding and recognizing team members
10. Providing a safe place to work
11. People management skills for managers
12. People management skills for managers of managers
13. Manager behaviors.

# Chapter 9

## Interpersonal Skills for Managers

*The use of good interpersonal skills (by everybody) provides the social glue to enable people to work together both constructively and productively.*

**AS PEOPLE ARE** *social beings and work is an environment where social interaction is required to achieve business outcomes*, the use of good interpersonal skills provides the "social glue" to enable people to work together. Good interpersonal skills, however, have limited value in a workplace and/or a working relationship which is otherwise flawed in its design or is subject to ineffective leadership.

Constructive working relationships require the right working environment. They require:

- The setting of expectations for all employees
- The defining of roles and role relationships
- Effective organizational design
- Effective systems of work
- A strong manager-employee working relationship, based on trust and fairness and delivered through effective managerial leadership

These design requirements are built into our model for constructive working relationships.

However, to perform their role well, managers do need to be proficient in certain interpersonal skills. Being a managerial leader is not about being charismatic, using charm, trading favors or relying on working the politics within an organization. Nor is it about building or sustaining personal friendships or social relationships, as these are an individual's private business and have nothing to do with an organization. Being a managerial leader is about having the skills to do your role and these skills can be learned.

The role of a manager is to *achieve the business goals set for them and at the same time, provide an environment that allows their team members to be effective and satisfied with their work while developing their full potential.* Therefore, interpersonal skills must support the delivery of this role, i.e. they must be grounded in the work content of the manager's role.

From the organization's perspective, the purpose of good interpersonal skills is about getting work done in a constructive and productive manner. Below are some guidelines that will support the development of constructive working relationships. While each topic is probably the subject of a book in and of itself, the aim here is to provide some general principles to get started.

## General Principles for Constructive Working Relationships

i.  Deliver the expectations of all employees (as outlined Chapter 4)

The *expectations of all employees* are designed to enable constructive working relationships. The delivery of these expectations is the starting point.

ii. In all working relationships, consistently demonstrate the behaviors required of all managers (as outlined in Chapter 8)

To create constructive working relationships, the focus should always be on the behaviors required by managers, i.e., honesty, integrity, respect, and collaboration. The aim is always to build and maintain trust. Honesty, integrity, and respect are essential ingredients to build the trust that enables productive work. In dealing with people always:

- Maintain or enhance self-esteem
- Focus on the problem — don't attack the person
- Respect the view of others. When differences in views or ideas occur, work first to understand the other person's perspective.
- Encourage team members to express their opinions and make suggestions.
- Allow team members adequate time to think through a problem and to suggest a solution.

iii.  Schedule time to build working relationships

Strong working relationships are grounded on a foundation of mutual trust and this can only be developed through interaction over time. All relationships need time to develop.
- Start by identifying the key stakeholders in your organization. Your team and stakeholders deserve extra time and attention.
- Endeavor to understand the needs of relationships. Are you clear about what you need from them? Do you know what they need from you? These needs should be defined in the role design and systems of work.
- Devote a portion of your day to laying the foundation of good relationships. Even five minutes a day, if it's genuine, can help to build a bond between you and a colleague. For example, you could pop into someone's office during lunch, before or after work. These little interactions help build the foundation of a good relationship, especially if they're face-to-face.
- Avoid gossip.

- When others provide assistance or support, express appreciation for it.

iv. Communicate openly and frequently

We communicate all day, whether we're sending emails, attending meetings or meeting face-to-face. Effective communication strategies can help build strong working relationships. Some general tips for good communications are:
- Respond to requests by emphasizing what you can do to help.
- Follow through and do what you say you'll do.
- Listen without passing judgment.
- Don't rush in to give advice.
- When you have concerns, work them out with the source, not with others.
- Communicate with respect in every interaction regardless of whether you like the person.
- Be direct and sincere as normal practice.
- Only use humor in good taste.
- Use active listening techniques, such as repeating back to the person who is talking what you heard him or her say. This assures that you are both on the same page.
- Communicate one-on-one or in small groups depending on the specific needs at the time.
- Ensure emails are clear, concise, to the point and respectful.
- When presenting to groups:
  o Provide backup material that is easy to read and to refer to, such as briefing cards.
  o Anticipate people's reactions and likely questions and plan accordingly.
  o Deal with rumors immediately and face-to-face.
  o Get feedback.

## Specific Principles for Constructive Working Relationships

When dealing with people, even the best managers will have things go wrong. The aim is to handle or resolve these issues honestly, respectfully and with integrity. Once again, the aim is to build trust. Trust in the system of management and trust in yourself, the manager.

i.   Addressing conflict

One of the most destructive situations in the workplace is the avoidance of or poor resolution of conflict. If left unattended, conflict is harmful and relationships will deteriorate over time. Conflict between individuals creates difficult working conditions for the people directly affected and those in the vicinity. If understood and properly confronted, the resolution of conflict usually improves the situation and the working relationship.

If a conflict is developing between a manager and a team member, the manager needs to recognize the signs of the conflict at an early stage and to confront the issues and resolve them. While the individual team member has a part to play, because of the manager's position of authority, the individual may not be inclined to address the issue or may leave it until it is too late.

The key principles of managing conflict are:
*   Note the occurrence of discomfort, reflect on its possible causes such as structure, unclear roles or role relationships (accountability and authority) or poor systems of work. Then decide what action, if any, to take.
*   If the conflict progresses to the next stage, then take action to recalibrate the relationship. At this stage, it may be an in-formal chat, and if this is seen as part of your normal response to a team member, it will be seen as a helpful and productive intervention.

Remember:

- o Maintain and enhance the self-esteem of the team member.
- o Don't attack the person. Focus on the problem or issue. Where necessary, provide a broader view, by giving more context to the situation.
- o Don't assume that the team member has committed an offense. Keep an open mind.
- o Seek to understand; ask the team member to explain their position and to make suggestions.
- o Keep the team's goals ahead of individual goals. This can help you stay focused.

- Allow adequate time for the team member to think through the problem. Help to work through issues, desired outcomes and options before anticipating the solution.
- Agree on an appropriate action plan.
- Always set a specific follow-up date.

ii.  Addressing unacceptable performance

There are times in a manager's role where they are required to address performance issues. When this occurs:

- Explain to the team member what you have observed and why it is unacceptable.
- Ask for and listen openly to the reasons which the team member offers for their behavior.
- State your requirements and guide the team member to formulate their program to meet these requirements.
- Offer your help to the team member to meet their requirements.
- Agree on the steps to be taken by each of you.
- If applicable, indicate what disciplinary steps will be taken and why.

iii.  Taking corrective action

When a performance issue has not been addressed, the manager may need to take corrective action. If this occurs:

- If applicable complement the team member on those aspects where some improvement has occurred or define the problem in terms of lack of improvement since the last meeting.
- Ask for and listen attentively to the team members reasons for lack of improvement.
- Decide whether more time should be granted to meet the required standards.
    - o  If yes, state your requirements and guide the team member to formulate a program to overcome the remaining obstacles. Agree on the steps to be taken by each of you and assure the team member of your continued desire to help them to succeed.
    - o  If no, either indicate what disciplinary action will be taken and why, or take the disciplinary action previously indicated.

iv.  Handling a complaint

When handling a complaint, it is important to:

- Listen attentively to the team member's complaint. Ensure you fully understand it.
- Show that you understand their feelings and thank them for raising the matter.
- State your own position without being defensive or hostile.
- Determine whether the team member has any suggestions for resolving their complaint.
- If applicable, specify what you will do to correct the situation.
- Set a follow-up date to review and discuss.

v. Introducing change

Part of the manager's role is to implement change in their team. The manager is accountable to lead, engage their team and enable the change in their team. When change occurs the manager must:

- Explain the conditions which have caused the need for change.
- Explain the detail of the change and how it will affect the person.
- Ask the person how they feel about the proposals, identify their major needs and concerns and recognize any new problems they may experience.
- If applicable, include a practical demonstration or teach the person how to carry out the new process.
- Ask their suggestions for:
  o Overcoming the problems
  o Implementing the change

vi. Recognizing good work

Part of building trust and a high performing team is to recognize good work. To make recognition effective managers must:

- Describe to the team member specifically what they did that deserves recognition and why.
- Express personal appreciation.
- Ask the person if there is anything you can do to make it easier for them to do their work.

Identifying and managing people issues are part of managerial work. The fast identification and quick resolution of conflict enable the development and continuation of constructive working relationships.

## Key Concepts

- The use of good interpersonal skills provides the "social glue" that enables people to work together constructively and productively. However, good interpersonal skills have limited value in a workplace and/or a working relationship which is otherwise flawed in its design or is subject to ineffective leadership.
- Whenever dealing with people, the aim is always to build and maintain trust. Some general principles are:
  o Deliver the expectations of all employees.
  o Consistently demonstrate the behaviors required of all managers.
  o Schedule time to build relationships.
  o Communicate openly and frequently.
- Identifying and managing people issues is part of managerial work. Specific requirements for managers when dealing with people is to handle or resolve these issues honestly, respectfully and with integrity. Once again, the aim is to build trust. Trust in the system of management and trust in yourself, the manager. Managers need specific skills to:
  o Address conflict
  o Address unacceptable performance
  o Take corrective action
  o Handle complaints Manage change
  o Recognize good work

## Tips for Getting Started

1. Get feedback on your managerial skills and behaviors. There are many tools around, so it is up to you. If you are a member of The Leadership Framework website, you can assess your managerial leadership skills using the *Manager Skills Self-Assessment*.

2. Once assessed, select an area for improvement. Members can read the relevant content on this site.
3. Create an action plan for improvement.

## Additional information available at www.theleadershipframework.com.au

1. Understanding yourself
2. People management skills for managers
3. People management skills for managers of managers
4. Manager behaviors
5. Manager Skills Self-Assessment (based on the Leadership Framework)
6. Manager of Manager Skills Self-Assessment (based on the Leadership Framework)
7. Short guide to managing relationships
8. Leading change
9. Understanding resistance to change

# Summary

**AT THE TIME** of writing this summary, I am reviewing a potential client's development program aimed at improving workplace productivity by improving collaboration both within and across teams. Once again, it is all about interpersonal skills. The program has nothing about creating an environment to enable constructive working relationships. There is nothing about structure, clear roles and role relationships or systems of work. There is nothing defining the importance of building strong, two-way working relationships based on trust. It is all about improving the attitudes and interpersonal skills of managers. In its current form, the program will not be successful in delivering the change they want. This skills program will very likely fail.

Collaboration and constructive working relationships are not about everyone being nice. It is about people working together in a positive manner, doing productive work to achieve organizational objectives. This requires the right workplace environment. An environment that creates the systemic trust that enables productive work. It requires a clear understanding of roles and role relationship as well as each role's accountabilities and authorities. These factors release people to work together. They empower people to do their best work.

It is the working environment that enables people to work together in a constructive manner. It is the working environment that shapes behavior.

## Model for Constructive Working Relationships

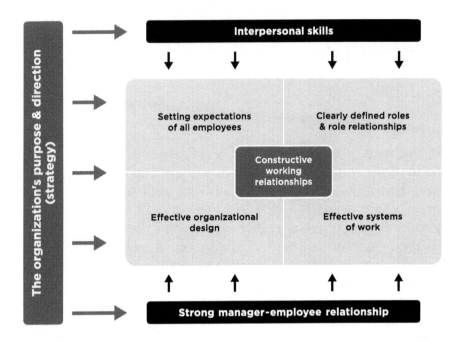

The model above encompasses all these requirements. To build constructive working relationships managers must:

i.   Set expectations of all employees

As with any social situation, there are rules or expectations of behavior on how people interact. Behavioral expectations will develop whether they are specified or not. Managers must set these expectations to achieve business outcomes in a constructive and productive way.

ii.   Design the organization's structure to enable productive work

The organization's design provides the shared understanding of accountability and authority that exists between people whose work is aligned and integrated to deliver the organization's purpose and direction. Effective design enables constructive working relationships, with clear accountability, while poor organizational design has the potential to create workplace conflict.

iii. Clearly define roles and role relationships

In organizations, there are different types of roles with different types of authority. Well designed roles, with clear accountabilities and authorities, provide the rules for engagement and enables focused thinking on the work to be done. They enable people to work together both constructively and productively, towards business goals. Clear roles, accountabilities with appropriate authorities, do not hinder work they empower people to do their work and to work together.

iv. Provide effective systems of work

Systems of work, such as policies and processes facilitate productive work; they enable people to work together. Systems of work create custom, practices, traditions, beliefs and assumptions which in turn create the organization's culture. Systems of work define what is valued in the organization by the senior leadership team.

v. Build strong manager-employee working relationships

The foundation of having constructive working relationships is the manager-employee relationship. A strong manager-employee working relationship can only be achieved when managers have strong, personally earned authority gained through effective performance in their role. The focus of this relationship is on achieving business goals. It is based on care, dignity, respect and mutual trust between the manager and each team member. It is critical to the success of both the manager and each team member. It is critical for the working relationships of the team.

vi.  Develop interpersonal skills

As people are social beings and work is an environment where social interaction is required to achieve business outcomes, managers need relationship management skills for dealing with people and managing issues. The development of these skills provides the social glue for the team to work together.

Building constructive working relationships requires a holistic approach. It requires a focus on the organization's purpose, structure, systems of work and managerial leadership, along with the symbols they create. These build and sustain an organization's culture. How they are designed and delivered, will enable or discourage people from working together.

## Learn More

Learn more on building constructive working relationships or The Leadership Framework by joining The Leadership Framework Network at www.theleadershipframework.com.au, either as an individual or organization and gain access to:

1.  Information, tools, templates, and checklists that will support you to create the constructive working environment that enables productive work.
2.  Additional information on how to:
    - Improve managerial leadership — at all levels
    - Create effective organization structures
    - Implement business strategy

- Improve workforce capability
- Identify and develop talent
- Improve safety performance
- Build effective teams and teamwork
- Build mutual trust and strong manager-employee working relationships
- Improve employee engagement
- Manage change
- Improve work systems and processes
- Manage performance issues.

Alternatively
1. Read *Leading People — The 10 Things Successful Managers Know and Do* by Peter Mills to gain a better understanding of the role, accountabilities and authorities of managers and how they can build and lead effective teams.
2. Arrange seminars/workshops on any aspect of the Leadership Framework.

# Appendix 1

## The Leadership Framework

### The Leadership Framework

**THE LEADERSHIP FRAMEWORK** provides managers and organizations with a complete, holistic and coherent system of managerial leadership. It considers the organization as a purpose-built structure, with systems of work and specifically designed working relationships that enable people to work towards a common business purpose. The organization itself is activated or deployed by applying effective managerial leadership.

The Leadership Framework describes what all managers must know and must do. It clearly defines the requirements for leadership and sets practical and consistent standards expected of people leaders. Being a holistic framework it can be used to:

- Improve managerial leadership — at all levels
- Implement business strategy
- Create effective organization structures
- Improve workforce capability
- Talent identification and development
- Improve safety performance
- Build effective teams and teamwork
- Build mutual trust and strong manager-employee relationships
- Improve employee engagement
- Manage change

- Improve work systems and processes
- Manage performance issues

The Framework's three interconnecting parts provide a set of integrated principles and practices for the organization and for the individual.

**Leading people**
1. Provide a safe working environment
2. Create effective roles & fill them with good people
3. Effectively assign & assess work
4. Develop team capability
5. Recognize & reward work
6. Build teamwork
7. Enable continuous improvement & lead change

**Leading yourself**
1. Understand your role
2. Understand & respect the role of others
3. Manage relationships
4. Develop important managerial leadership skills & behaviors
5. Apply the framework

**Leading the organization**
1. Implement business strategy
2. Design the organization
3. Design & maintain productive systems of work
4. Enable systemic trust & fairness
5. Build workforce capability
6. Manage strategic relationships

**Leading yourself** is about understanding the role of the manager and how to work with others across the organization, building quality working relationships. It also comprises the essential requirements of what managers need to know about how to deal productively with workplace conflict and people differences.

**Leading people** is about the things managers must do on a day-to-day basis to manage their team. It comprises the minimum and essential requirements of all people managers from frontline managers up to, and including, the CEO/managing director. It includes creating effective roles and filling them with good people, assigning and assessing work, rewarding and recognizing good work, building a capable team, continuous improvement and managing change and providing a safe place to work.

**Leading the organization** is about the additional requirements of managers occupying roles immediately above the frontline manager level. It involves designing and implementing fit for purpose workplace conditions such as organizational structures and systems of work to enable and support effective managerial leadership and productive work. Business strategy and building workforce capability is part of this.

At the framework's core are strong, two-way, trusting, working relationships, focused on achieving business goals.

Using The Leadership Framework enables organizations to operate effectively to deliver strategy. It enables managers to build high-performing teams focused on achieving business objectives. It also enables managers to develop team members to their full potential and be personally successful.

## Origin of The Leadership Framework

At the framework's foundation is a body of knowledge known as *Requisite Organization*, requisite meaning what is required by the natural order of things. The concepts and principles were originally developed by Dr. Elliott Jaques and Lord Wilfred Brown and are based on significant research and practice around the world. This research considers organizational design as a purpose-built structure, with systems of work and defined working relationships that enable people to work toward a common business purpose. The organization itself is activated by applying effective managerial leadership practices.

The original Leadership Framework was developed by Barry and Sheila Deane, from PeopleFit Australasia, who simplified and condensed Jaques' principles and practices.

Using PeopleFit's work, I have complemented, modified and updated it using the research of others and from my own extensive experience:

- In senior human resources' roles across a range of industries both in the private and public sector
- In working directly with my own team as a leader on setting goals and improving performance
- As an advisor and coach to CEOs, managers, and non-manager roles in organizations

The Leadership Framework is the only complete framework for people management.

Printed in Australia
AUOC01n1132250417
285005AU00005B/5/P